OUTSIDE BROADCASTER

OUTSIDE BROADCASTER

ERIC ROBSON

FRANCES LINCOLN LIMITED

PUBLISHERS

TO NESSIE AND JIMMY

Frances Lincoln Ltd
4 Torriano Mews
Torriano Avenue
London NW5 2RZ
www.franceslincoln.com

A catalogue record for this book is available from
the British Library.

ISBN 13: 978-0-7112-2779-8

Printed and bound in China

1 3 5 7 9 8 6 4 2

CONTENTS

CHAPTER ONE
DODGY MEMORIES

I t was catalepsy that did it.

To be more precise, one evening in the bar of The Screes Hotel in Nether Wasdale in the Lake District, it took me four hours to remember the word catalepsy. I realised I'd better get something down on paper before it all became unrecoverable. Over the years I've known parties at the Screes so wild that they could bring on very similar symptoms to catalepsy – the prolonged rigid posture of people appearing dead enough to be buried while still being technically alive.

This wasn't such a party. This was an intimation of senility.

It was a typical Lakeland spring evening. A steady, grey downpour was slowly obliterating views of the Wastwater screes. A couple of sad walkers were steaming and gibbering in a corner, clutching their half-pints of lager for warmth. Bill, on the Father of the House barstool in the corner, was the letters page of the *Daily Telegraph* made flesh with the usual, entirely reasonable grumbles about self-serving politicians, unwatchable television programmes and barmy European directives. David the headmaster was, as ever, digging his escape tunnel from the education service. And there was me, the local freelance broadcaster, taking a night off from filling in the ethnic diversity and risk assessment forms that are the creative essence of modern television production. At the far end of the bar Nick, the landlord, was glazing over as the other television man present – John the TV repair man – set about rewriting the history of the war in the Pacific yet again. Perhaps this time Japan would win.

'Shut up, John. Nick looks as if he's suffering from . . .'

At which point I couldn't remember the word.

'Haemorrhoids?'

'Tony Blair's libertarian policies?'

'Post-traumatic stress disorder?'

'Drinking the beer he sells?'

All useful suggestions from the assembled company, but not the word that was tickling about on the end of my tongue, refusing to emerge.

'I'm sure it begins with a C-A . . .'

'Camping?' suggested the ample female walker in the corner, who by now had warmed up enough to regain the power of speech. She pulled off two layers of sodden walking gear.

Cleavage. Consternation. Cornucopia.

I went home.

Catarrh. Epilepsy. Necrophilia.

It just wouldn't come.

And then, later in the evening, I happened to switch on BBC 1 and caught the highlights of the Queen Mother's Lying in State. Inspiration comes at the oddest moments. David Dimbleby was in full flow.

'. . . above us the hammer beams of history. Below a scene of almost imperial splendour. Flags and candlelight reflecting from the burnished uniforms of the honour guard. It's a scene that suggests little has changed since Queen Victoria's day. But, of course, we know it bloody well should have done, and I'm not going to pander to anachronistic monarchical sentiments by pretending otherwise . . .'

He didn't say that but you knew he was wishing he could. Professionally I've always found Dimbles rather suspect ever since he chattered on air during the national two minute silence on Remembrance Sunday. But, in fairness, perhaps he thought that as a Dimbleby he was exempt. Occasionally he can be brilliant. His description at one state occasion of a particularly bored Prince Philip looking like Count Dracula was spot on. I wish I'd thought of it. I will one day.

'. . . and at the centre of this sombre tableau of light and deep shadow the catafalque . . .'

'That's it. Catalepsy.'

'No, she's really dead,' said my wife, Annette, as she hurried by to rescue dinner from the incinerator.

When I told her later that evening that I was thinking of writing this book, her response was characteristically blunt and sensible.

'Don't.'

CHAPTER TWO
POTTY AND TRAINING

A pparently one symptom of incipient catalepsy is that you easily forget good advice.

Broadcasting wasn't part of the original plan. My only contact with it was the Radio Luxembourg world of Dan Dare entered through the bamboo box with faintly glowing yellow dials that was my grandfather's Ferguson radio. Sitting in a darkened room, tucked up in a red dressing gown and sipping a cup of Horlicks – compulsory because Horlicks sponsored the programme – as Dan fought off the evil invaders. Kids like me, born in those far-off days in the little village of Newcastleton in Roxburghshire, probably had as much chance of bumping into the Mekong as of strolling into Broadcasting House.

I'd been born after a lengthy labour on New Year's Eve 1946 in the back bedroom of my grandparents' house in Douglas Square. My parents – Nessie, the station-master's daughter, and Jimmy, a local authority fireman – were gentle people. Dad had experienced all the excitement he needed in life in the five years he'd spent as a prisoner of war. The nail-biting detail of his eventual escape from the POW camp by hiding in a roof void to wait for the brief breathing space between German retreat and Russian advance, his trek by night across Eastern Europe to Odessa, the refusal of an American ship to let him on board, and the blunt, Scottish Borders-style smack in the mouth for an American sentry which got him thrown in the brig just as the ship was about to sail for Greenock was a tale that took him almost thirty years to tell.

My own experience of life just after the war was considerably less troubled. I most definitely remember being three. I would pedal off on my repainted, second-hand Christmas tricycle each afternoon to take Annie Jardine's three milking cows from their cobwebbed backstreet byre with its pails of steaming milk to their grazings on the hill overlooking the village. It never occurred to me, as they ambled and I whooped and waved a hazel twig, that they knew the way better than me. I thought I was a proper farmer. Forty years later I would try to be one again.

My grandmother, Annie, obviously predicted long before any television set flickered to life in Newcastleton that repetitive, tasteless cookery programmes were going to be a staple of British broadcasting. In the Douglas Square kitchen she started teaching me how to cook at the age of three. By four I'd mastered any number of puddings, shepherd's pie and basic breadmaking. By the age of forty I realised she'd made a fundamental mistake. It was only if I couldn't cook or was too bloody idle to try that I could get onto one of those shows.

My grandfather, Simon – known universally as Simmon – had been the North British Railway stationmaster at Newcastleton. In his company I learned the commonplaces of steam locomotion. An excited little boy lofted into the cab of gleaming and wheezing machines – Mallard once – which I'd drive to the far signal by touching a chubby finger to a valve or a lever. I was then set down on the lineside to toddle home, my greasy hand in Simmon's. Just imagine running those joyous childhood experiences past the Health and Safety Executive today.

By the time I was four there was already a strange theatrical connection in my life. In Simmon's front room, which doubled as his JP's office, I'd meet the barnstormers who turned up at certain seasons of the year to book the village hall and get a performance licence. They'd bring 'a wee something for the grandbairn', presumably in the hope of getting the hiring fee knocked down a bit. One of the presents was a model of a great ocean liner made of cardboard with cotton wool smoke in its funnels. It sailed the top landing of the house in Douglas Square for some years, until it was blown out of the water by a wind-up Massey Ferguson tractor the day its spring went haywire.

But the real delight of those occasional meetings was peeping round a sofa end, watching and listening to the threadbare thespians with funny hair, booming voices and rheumy eyes outlining the plots of their melodramas and pantomimes. A quarter of a century later, I met one of them again while I was working as a regional television reporter. Elliot Williams must have been pushing eighty by then. I swear he was still wearing the same improbable wig he'd had on in my grandfather's office all those years before. A wig that had the disconcerting habit of being entirely independent of his head. When he turned, it didn't. But he was still every bit the booming, old-style actor manager putting on tatty but cheerful semi-professional productions of *Murder in the Red Barn* in village halls in the Scottish Borders.

I didn't know it at the time, but the whiff of greasepaint and whisky was going to linger. In the meantime, I had a few years of overcoming profound shyness and learning to live with the entirely appropriate nickname of Fatty Robson.

By my early teenage years, and by then living in the metropolis of Carlisle, I'd taken to the theatre with a vengeance. And most of the vengeance was my long-suffering mother's as she manfully tried to persuade me not to stay out at rehearsals till two in the morning. I can still vividly remember the first time I went backstage at Her Majesty's Theatre as a trainee assistant stage manager's gopher for a local Gilbert and Sullivan production. The grammar school had been asked to supply some free labour by the local impresario Lionel Lightfoot, solicitor by day, actor manager after dark. The dim lighting in the wings reinforced the sense of mystery of the place. Ropes disappeared upwards into a black void from which would come painted scenes of glory. In reality they were tatty backdrops that, close up, looked as if they'd been daubed by a drunken scene painter let loose with a six-inch brush devoid of bristles. But from the dress-circle they made magic. And to this day I can still conjure up the smell of Leichner 5 and 9, the greasy sticks of flesh-tone make-up that turned a rather shy little boy into the Duke of Clarence, Prospero or the third spear carrier from the left. I learned early how easy it was to suspend disbelief. Later, as my broadcasting career got into what passed for its stride, I began to realise that a substantial part of the audience was prepared to suspend critical judgement as well.

Shortly after my undistinguished debut at Her Majesty's, Carlisle Council pulled the place down to underline its commitment to the arts in the city. As I write some forty years later, the site, which at the time was vital for development to ensure the city's economic well-being, is still a temporary car park. But with Her Majesty's gone, I had to find another outlet for my unproven dramatic talents.

I found one at the subterranean Green Room Club. It may have been a cockroach-infested cellar with a stage the size of a back bedroom, but it, too, made magic. Eight or nine productions a year in which I acted and stage managed, built sets and, in the cramped backstage corridors, had my first experience of girls in various stages of undress. Just as well, really. A spot of juvenile backstage lust at least helped to ward off adolescent confusion.

Carlisle Grammar was a boys' school so we fresh-faced juniors had to play the female parts in school plays. That meant we were encouraged to have a potentially unhealthy interest in female undergarments from an early age. At rehearsals masters would be warning of the dangers of sexual diversity in one breath and urging us to hitch up our bras in the next. In fact, there was a spell when appearing in school plays meant I was probably wearing a bra more regularly than the girls at the high school down the road. Bras were banned there (even for particularly well-developed pupils) for fear they would emphasise the temptations on offer. The same reasoning insisted on regulation blue knickers. Now, serge pants may have had the bromide effect the staff of the high school intended, but untrammelled sways and undulations most certainly did not.

Perhaps as a reaction to their stricter rules, the girls seemed to grow up much faster than the boys as we fumbled our way into the 1960s. They had a clearer idea of what was what, where and when. Experimentation benefited from their tuition. I never have been able to remember where I was when President Kennedy was shot, but I can remember every pneumatic detail of the back row of the Lochinvar Picture House in Longtown, and the Harry Houdini challenge of practising the total undressing of a spectacularly well-constructed and single-minded girl in the front seat of a Triumph Spitfire – a challenge that took several enjoyable weeks to get right. Another appealing feminine trait I discovered in those days was boundless patience when faced with incompetence.

The years at the Green Room Club provided more innocent pleasures, too. Pantomimes taken on tour to remote village halls. One evening, the company arrived in the hamlet of Mungrisedale on the edge of the Caldbeck Fells in a blizzard and a power cut. The only way they could do the performance was by leaving the hall's double doors open and lighting the stage with the headlamps of the bus that carried the scenery. The audience was fine, muffled up to just below the eyes in scarves and overcoats. The skimpily clad ladies of indeterminate age in the gypsy chorus almost froze to death. We took the same production to the Congregational church hall in Carlisle, where at least there was light and warmth, but that didn't help poor Winnie Fisher, our gypsy accordionist. She would go in front of the curtains and play jolly musical medleys while we changed the scenery. Unfortunately, nobody had noticed that at the church hall there wasn't anything in front of the curtains except the orchestra pit. The last we heard of Winnie was the strangled-cat cry of a plunging accordion and a discordant crash of cymbal and roll of snare as she landed in the drum kit. But she got a tremendous round of applause.

And there were more serious ventures. At the grammar school I co-produced one of the first amateur productions of *Waiting for Godot*. My Estragon to Keith Klein's Vladimir. Keith was a proper actor. He was gay. But less happy words were used about him at the time. *Godot* took six months to get right, and I suspect the varnished school stage still hasn't recovered from the five tons of ballast and two railway lines that comprised the set. Certainly the headmaster at the time, a kindly man who looked like a skull on legs, the double of Prime Minister Sir Alec Douglas Home, was unimpressed by having to conduct school assembly on a heap of rubble for some weeks.

Godot, is, of course, one of the great plays of modern times, but what I remember most clearly about the production is not its existentialist message but the moment I sat on a box of matches which exploded. As my trousers smouldered, my backside charred and I was enveloped in a cloud of acrid smoke, my next line – perfectly delivered – was, 'I suppose I'll get up under my own steam in the fullness of time.' The audience marvelled at the timing, but I fear Samuel Beckett would have disapproved of the laughter it generated.

There was serious work going on at the Green Room Club as well, and most of it involved Norman Johnston. He was a prodigious talent who worked for the Water Board. No, that's not strictly true. He was paid by the Water Board, but his day job was bringing radical new theatrical experiences to audiences in Carlisle that weren't quite ready for them yet. Among those plays was *Afore Night Come* by David Rudkin. I think it was its amateur premiere. It's a story of superstition and fear set in a Midlands pear orchard during which one of the itinerant harvesters, a tramp called Shakespeare, has to be beheaded on stage. As the front row of the audience could put their feet on the stage at the Green Room Club, it was a tricky bit of action to pull off. Norman commissioned a wonderfully lifelike replica of the actor's head. After the beheading, it was rolled down the stage and used as a football. On the first night two members of the audience were sick. But the head had its most dramatic impact on the young bobby who stopped Norman on the way home from rehearsals late one night and demanded to know what was in his holdall. One severed head and four blood-covered pruning knives later, he was spark out on the pavement of West Walls.

By the age of eighteen my theatrical lunacies knew no bounds. Between last-minute spurts of school work I was directing the Carlisle Arts Festival, and managed to inspire such profound confidence in the organising committee that they resigned en bloc. The festival lost £22,000 which I had to find, and bankruptcy was averted only by the intervention of Harold Crowe, the bank manager, who bailed me out because he 'liked to see somebody having a go', a phrase that for some reason seems to have been dropped from the manual of good banking practice.

Maybe Harold was impressed that I was already running a book business while still in the lower sixth. A schoolmate, Ian Scott-Parker, and I took it in turns to skive on Tuesday (or was it Thursday?) afternoons to go to the sales at David King's auction rooms. When all the worthwhile stuff had gone under the hammer, they'd get round to the books – boxes full of them, baby baths overflowing with them which we picked up for ten bob a lot. We then hauled them up the rickety stair to our office in Tower Buildings, where they'd be sorted into junk, almost junk, valuable and textbooks. Valuable books went to the dealers and the junk went to Carlisle's equivalent of Fagin, who ran a seedy second-hand shop. But textbooks were the real prize. The grammar school charged pupils if they lost one. New price at that. We discovered that dozens of them turned up in the auctions so we could offer them at bargain prices. Apart from the handsome profit, it was particularly satisfying when we could take a pound or two from the macho rugby fraternity who had more success with the girls than Ian and I, who both had a tendency to run to fat and idleness.

Meanwhile, during my occasional non-theatrical appearances at school, Adrian Barnes was doing his unflustered best to keep me in the paths of righteousness. He failed but that was because I was unredeemable. Adrian was the senior English master, aristocratic and handsome, who processed through the school in a measured billow of black gown, a cloud of chalk dust and a miasma of minty vapours. He had the capacity to take Chaucer, Shakespeare or Robert Browning and make them as vibrant to a bunch of uniformed degenerates as was *The Eagle* comic and, later, *Penthouse* magazine. But, better than that, he was on our side.

One lunchtime a group of us – none older than 15 – wandered into the front lounge of the Central Hotel in Carlisle in the hope of finding a short-sighted barman who would miss the fact we were all dressed in our distinctive black and yellow school blazers while pouring us our pints of bitter. We were three feet from the door when a voice boomed from the bar counter and silenced all conversation.

'Find your own bar, boys.'

We scurried, and on our way to the Appletree agreed that we really should apologise to Adrian for our lack of consideration when we saw him for the first period after lunch.

Better still, Adrian, then in his late forties or early fifties, ran off with the art mistress, the very beautiful Mrs Cooper. Now that's a proper teacher. I kept in touch with him until he died, and I still see June, who continues to paint with abandon. But, sadly, not even Adrian managed to divert me from the crazy-paved path that I'd been following since the Carlisle Festival.

Once bitten twice as stupid. As if the Festival losses weren't bad enough, impresarial tendencies blossomed. Two or three of us decided it would be a great idea to bring the Century Theatre from Keswick to play a winter season on a windswept car park by Carlisle Castle. The theatre had been founded a quarter of a century earlier to take the theatrical experience to remote rural communities. Circus-like, it folded out of four articulated lorries which, having been parked up in Keswick for a decade, were so decrepit they needed a police escort for the entire journey. That should have given us a clue. The Century's arrival in Carlisle and its temporary renaming as the Centurion Theatre coincided with a month of torrential rain. We couldn't sell seats in rows eleven to fourteen because they were full of buckets catching the drips. Not that the loss of four rows was a burden. Audiences were so small that most nights we had more buckets than people anyway. We did, however, manage to get a fair amount of national publicity, most notably a full page with photographs in the *Daily Express* about the night someone was doing a one-man show called 'No Man is an

Island' and the audience comprised just two usherettes. I can't remember the actor's name, but he was nothing if not professional. He went ahead with the performance and bought an ice cream from one of his audience in the interval.

It goes without saying that by the time the theatre was folded back onto its ancient lorries to limp back to Keswick, the venture had lost prodigious sums of money. But at least this time they were underwritten by grants. I wouldn't have to throw myself on Harold Crowe's mercy again.

Chaotic, exciting and with a limited grip on financial reality, it was all a perfect grounding for working in the BBC. The careers master who was trying to persuade me of the challenging delights of a job in teaching or accountancy didn't stand a chance. But I did miss a trick. My history master, Spike Morlin, once gave me a bit of advice that I stupidly ignored. Holding my inadequate history homework between thumb and forefinger as if it was infected with MRSA, he said, 'Ropson, have you never considered an alternative career in plum-bing?' Had I known then that plumbers in London can reputedly earn seventy-five quid an hour, I might have taken his suggestion more seriously.

CHAPTER THREE
THE BREAK

I ended up in broadcasting because my mother was sick of me squandering a grammar school education by working as a furniture remover for Pickfords. My parents still wanted me to be a teacher or some such. I wanted to be an actor. Walking backwards while carrying a wardrobe was my idea of a compromise.

Quite how many jobs my mother secretly applied for on my behalf I'm not sure, but she had to own up when her application to Border Television got me an interview. The job on offer was Assistant to the Head of Presentation and I didn't want it. I was quite happy as a furniture remover – a fascinating job that shows people at their very worst, moving house being second only to bereavement in the scale of human horrors. And I'd mastered the skills. How to find the kettle on a crammed furniture van, how to make everyone else walk backwards while carrying the heavy end of the wardrobe, and how to busy myself untangling securing straps when the moment came to get the piano onto the second floor.

My attitude at the Border TV interview was a blend of haughty amusement and relaxed resignation at having to waste an hour of lucrative furniture moving time on a Thursday afternoon. Naturally I got the job. Demonstrating what everyone else must have seen as the arrogance of youth, but which I reckoned at the time was plain common sense, I said

I'd only take it if they would guarantee me a job in television production in two years. The ploy didn't work. They agreed and the following Monday morning I had to begin learning a whole new set of skills with the help of Maureen and Sylvia in the programme schedules office.

By lunchtime they'd taught me how to book transmission circuits and everything I didn't want to know about menstruation. By knocking off time I'd blushed more in one day than in eighteen months with the centrefold pin-ups and dirty jokes of Pickfords. In about a fortnight they had me broken in. Housetrained as they preferred to put it. I could collect their morning coffee from the canteen without spilling a drop, and at the same time remember that Sylvia preferred marmalade on her cheese scone. I disappeared without a quibble when they told me that Gwynne, the vision mixer, wanted to come to the office for a private, girls-only chat. I was never short of an excuse to explain to the boss why they weren't back from lunch at half past two. I got to enjoy it. Away from the office I proudly told people that I was working in television.

One of my administrative jobs, when I could find time away from the canteen queue, was to handle viewers' complaints and requests.

'Dear Sir, will you tell that Ena Sharples woman on *Coronation Street* that it's the height of bad manners to be seen in her night hairnet in the pub?'

'No.'

'Dear Sir, what does Border Television mean by having two items on the news from Selkirk last night and none from Carlisle?'

'It means there wasn't any news in Carlisle yesterday.'

I thought I was quite good at it.

Some of the requests needed a more diplomatic response, like the one from the secretary of a Women's Institute somewhere in the Scottish Borders who wrote to ask if she could bring a coach load of ladies down to Carlisle to watch the next recording of *Bonanza*.

'Sorry, we've had to postpone *Bonanza* recordings because the gunfire and horses were disturbing the bakery workers who share the trading estate with us, and the residents of the Harraby estate across the road have complained to the council.'

Having sent that reply, I worried that I'd been a bit heavy on the sarcasm until the WI secretary wrote back by return thanking me for my letter and hoping we'd bear her request in mind when we'd sorted the problem out and started recording again. To this day, whenever some TV producer proudly boasts about how many millions of people have watched, enjoyed and understood his programme, I think of that WI secretary.

By some oversight, Carlisle has never appeared in any media history. But in my early days there, it was positively bursting with talent. I still have a photograph from one of my early school plays of the chorus of poor women of Canterbury from *Murder in the Cathedral*. Apart from a very pretty and headscarved E. Robson, there's the coquettish Roger Bolton, who became Margaret Thatcher's least favourite documentary maker after *Death on the Rock*, and the Rubenesque Roger Liddle, who went on to become a mouthpiece for the Liberal Democrats and an advisor to Tony Blair, a career briefly halted when he allowed his mouth to offer preferential access to senior politicians – allegedly. The same school had recently nurtured two considerable literary talents – Hunter Davies and Reg Hill, the creator of Dalziel and Pascoe. Not a bad tally for a rather faded squirearchy grammar school.

By this stage I'd left home in search of independence. My dad was slighted and didn't speak to me for almost a year – a rift that, when it was healed, turned us into the best of friends until the day he died. If he'd been aware of just how uncomfortable

I was in those first months away from the nest, it would probably have cheered him up no end. My first billet was a caravan on a campsite near Carlisle. I moved in on a bitterly cold January day. After a long struggle with the coke stove, there was a volcanic whoosh and every therm disappeared up the chimney. When I woke up the next morning, my beard was frozen to the bedclothes, the cups were encased in a block of ice in the washing up bowl, and my girlfriend was in the grip of advanced hypothermia.

I moved out and found a flat in a draculaic country house appropriately called The Knells. There would undoubtedly have been ghosts if they could have survived the temperature. I soon realised that being forced to wear long johns and thermals was a barrier to sexual excess and set out in search of central heating. I found it thanks to a continuity announcer from Border TV called Mary Winters, who offered me a spare room in her splendid rented flat in the posh suburb of Stanwix. Its owners had let it fully furnished – antiques, silverware, the lot. This was how broadcasters really should be living. Unfortunately, Mary's parties, which were legendary, weren't doing a lot of good to the aforementioned antiques, and the final straw was when she started to keep her pet white mice in the grand piano. The fear of possible reparations encouraged me to look for somewhere more in keeping with my lowly status – a student slum.

The flat I found near the Border studios was a nest of aspiring communicators. There was a chap on the top floor whose name I can't remember, if indeed I ever knew it, who locked himself in a bedroom decorated entirely in matt black, piled high with empty lager cans. He created artworks of such horror and lack of talent that he's probably now feted by the arts establishment if not a winner of the Turner Prize. A neighbour was Bea Campbell, whose writing blended feminism and Orwell in a powerful broth of ideas, and a regular visitor was Mike Hollingsworth in the days long before he became Mr Anne Diamond. When I first met him he was working as an aspiring newsman with a local press agency. Here he spent long days of investigative journalism scouring every regional newspaper to find the single-column-inch snippets that were flogged on to the *Sunday Post*. While all these people were busily advancing their careers, I'd gone back to labouring.

The management at Border TV had been as good as their word. After eighteen months or so, they suggested I apply for a vacancy as assistant floor manager, which was then a stepping stone to studio director, and counted as the production job I'd stuck out for at the initial interview. Suddenly I was back at Pickfords, only this time I was humping scenery. Unfortunately, Harry Leyland and Charlie Weeds, the studio scenehand and props man, were better than I'd ever been at making people walk backwards while carrying the heavy end of the set.

When I started floor managing, Border was still transmitting live commercial breaks between live programmes. (I should explain that the floor manager is the efficient link between the director in the gallery and the performers in the studio – at least that's the theory.) So having done the news programme, a lady in one corner of the studio would chat for two or three minutes about bargain baked beans on sale at a particular local supermarket while those of us on the scene crew took out the news set, revealing the set for the following programme behind it. As you can imagine, the potential for disaster was always just around the corner and quite regularly arrived, particularly if the following programme involved live sheep, which many of Border's programmes seemed to do in those days. Imagine the scene. The baked bean lady is in full flow, at which point a sheep wanders through the bottom of frame with Charlie Weeds on hands and knees in hot pursuit. It wouldn't have been quite so bad if, just behind the lady, Charlie hadn't looked up to see where the sheep had gone. It appeared for all the world as if he'd just emerged from under her skirt. Viewers inevitably drew their own conclusions about why the saleswoman had been so enervated and chirpy for the last couple of minutes. But a triumphant cry from Charlie and a strangled bleat from the sheep probably distracted potential purchasers from registering the exact price of the bargain beans.

Eventually I was allowed to floor manage programmes on my own. Epilogues. If you don't remember epilogues, they were those three or four minute slices of jollified religion (they were grimmer if it was the Church of Scotland's turn) that went out at midnight just before the white dot when nobody was watching. They allowed ITV to claim it was a public service broadcaster. And I'm happy to be able to remind you of those halcyon days when television used to stop at midnight and we had to think of other ways of filling in the small hours.

From epilogues I progressed to programme inserts: batches of recordings –perhaps ten a day – that were kept in the library to fill thin news days. Which, of course, were most days in the Border patch. We had a chef, Toni Stoppani, who would whip up spectacular delicacies on a temporary gas cooker in a rather shaky chipboard kitchen assembled in the studio. After setting the odd casserole on fire, we called him Stromboli after the volcano. He was immensely popular and would have been even more so had the audience realised how often he dropped 'the one we made earlier' as he was taking it out of the oven. We would stop recording. I would shovel the casserole contents into another dish, glass and all. Toni would rearrange the topping and then smile contentedly as he tasted it on camera. We couldn't hold the shot for long, because he had to spit it out if he wasn't going to shred his digestive tract.

Then there was the fortune-teller, a sort of sub Mystic Meg, who regularly forgot that she was supposed to be at the studio on Wednesdays. Having eventually clattered onto the set in a chaos of gypsy accoutrements and crystal balls, she would set about telling the region's Leos and Capricorns that they faced a truly horrible week during which they were likely to fall under a bus at the very least. CUT. I'd explain to her that sending waves of panic through the audience wasn't really what we hoped she'd do. No problem. Take two.

'With Saturn in the ascendancy and Venus in close proximity, Leos and Capricorns can expect a really successful few days with the prospect of a new job and a holiday to be won.'

Well, that's all right then. As I remember it, her catch phrase used to be 'think lucky and you'll be lucky', but she can't have been thinking hard enough because she didn't have her contract renewed.

And there were the musicians – for so they described themselves – who were either one-time minor stars who had hit the bottle or newcomers who had a career of alcoholism stretching ahead of them if they didn't take Charlie Weeds's no doubt well-meant advice to get a job stacking shelves at Woolworths. As I used to tell Charlie, he could probably have helped their performance and career prospects greatly if he hadn't given them his verdict until after the recording.

If the inserts were bad, some of the programmes were worse. In those days Border TV made just one series for the network, a cheap meringue of a programme called *Mr and Mrs* presented by one-time ventriloquist Derek Batey, who – between bursts of forced laughter – would ask excruciating questions aimed at finding out how much married couples really knew about each other. Someone once described Derek to me as having all the character and depth of Formica but, of course, formica was all the rage at the time. His sign-off line at the end of every episode was an emetic 'be nice to one another'. He then retreated to the company boardroom to hatchet the contestants who'd gone home and chat up one of the show's low-cut hostesses.

Fortunately, there were other, larger than life characters around who made floor managing a thoroughly enjoyable and varied job. One of the programme directors, Brian Izzard, was outrageously camp and creative in equal measure. He had a habit of throwing television sets and typewriters out of his first-floor office window, and occasionally he'd threaten to throw his secretary after them when she made the mistake of complaining he was going over budget. Brian was once stopped by the police in his car on the way to a party dressed as a nun. It was said of him that he once went to an appointment at the VD clinic at Carlisle hospital in his distinctive car while wearing a brown paper bag over his head. But that may be apocryphal. Brian also caused much damage. For one programme he demanded to have a steam-roller as part of the set. It was banned from the studio on the quite reasonable grounds that it would sink into the rubberised floor. Not to be beaten, he had it driven into the car park instead, where it promptly disappeared through the tarmac into the studio's main drainage system.

Brian thought I was a prat, mainly but not exclusively because I was union shop steward for the Association of Cinematograph, Television and Allied Technicians at the time. He believed the union's main aim in life was to thwart his creative processes. He was wrong. The main aim of the union was to thwart any creative process, wherever it might be found. Spats with management accumulated by the week. At one stage there were 72 unresolved disputes, and you could scarcely get into reception at Border for the heaps of new equipment that had been bought by the company but which the unions refused to install or operate until they got more money. During one national television strike (they were usually planned in the run-up to Christmas to cause maximum disruption to advertisers and company revenue, but this one was so urgently acrimonious that it was held in high summer), Border stayed out for another week after the rest of the ITV network had gone back to work. It had an extra demand – merely the sacking of the Managing Director. Looking back, it's amazing we managed to get any programmes on the air at all. But we did and some of them were surprisingly good fun to work on.

When Kevin Sheldon arrived from Ireland to produce late night folk music programmes, he was a breath of fresh Bushmills. He devised productions that might just have fitted into one of the big studios at BBC Television Centre in London, but would have needed one of Alice in Wonderland's magic lozenges to fit into Studio 1 at Carlisle. When I suggested, rather nervously, after the first live transmission of his folk music programme, *One Evening of Late*, that it was impossible for the cameramen and floor managers to stay out of shot, Kevin paused, stroked his old, grey, druid beard and offered us all method-acting lessons so we could more convincingly pretend we were part of the folk club scene. I dressed like a refugee from Woodstock for some months.

My boss was the cheery Harry King, who I suspect from the age of five had looked like a budding impresario in the Lew Grade mould. The two of us became great friends and played at show biz, helping out whenever we could get anywhere near the roar of the greasepaint. Humping scenery for the Acker Bilk band, operating the follow spots for Oscar Peterson, discovering local performers who were going to take the charts by storm but never did.

But then came the day when I made my first ever planned television appearance. In case it's slipped your mind, it was in a programme called *As Good as New*. The presenter of this canter through all things antique was a charming and statesmanlike chap called Alick Cleaver, who had a taste for gin and an outrageous handlebar moustache through which to strain it. He'd started his career as a cub reporter in somewhere like Leamington Spa, and when sufficiently down the bottle (which could be anytime after half past eleven in the morning) would tell the tale of his most memorable piece of court reporting – the case of a man who was being prosecuted for gross indecency with a duck. 'Well, bless my life and soul and I'll go to the foot of my stairs' was his inevitable punch line.

Alick also used to present the Saturday afternoon *Border Sports Report*. He would arrive from his garden in Burgh by Sands wearing wellies and a sweater which was quietly unravelling in the middle of his chest after an encounter with a rose bush. The wellies weren't a problem. They were under the desk. But, as duty floor manager, I had to tell Alick that the sweater was beyond the pale even for Border's easy-going presentation style. He took it off, put it on back to front revealing what looked like the aftermath of a creosote attack – and I gave up the unequal struggle.

Anyhow, Alick was doing an item on his antiques programme about mediaeval armour, and as the budget was non-existent the only available model was the assistant floor manager. I can confirm without fear of contradiction that the mediaeval fighting man was considerably smaller than his modern equivalent. For some weeks I carried the rivet marks and impaired circulation to prove it. Mercifully, the suit of armour I was asked to wear had lost its codpiece at Agincourt.

This first painful foray into the world of broadcasting celebrity would perhaps have deterred a more sensible person, but when I rang my mother that night I told her that I'd had my first big break. Sadly, I was only half-joking.

Soon after, there was a vacancy for a reporter on the local news programme, and having no journalistic experience whatsoever, naturally I applied. I was surprised when I didn't get the job. It went instead to a female reporter of doubtful provenance. What she apparently hadn't put on her CV was that she was about to star in one of those divorce cases to which only the *Daily Telegraph* can do full justice. 'She Wouldn't Wash My Socks; He Wouldn't Give Me Sex, Say TV Divorce Couple', sort of thing. The salacious detail may have done no end of good for the flagging libidos of breakfast table brigadiers, but it wasn't going to do a great deal for a certain reporter's career at Border TV. Invited to resign, the new reporter proceeded with all speed to the parapet of the bridge over the River Eden in the middle of Carlisle and threatened to jump if Border's Managing Director, James Bredin, didn't come and talk her down.

I should explain that being a Samaritan in the rain in front of the assembled local press was not Jim Bredin's idea of the perfect way to spend a Tuesday morning. Despite having had one of the top jobs at ITN and being the person credited with inventing *News at Ten*, he was a strangely reclusive man, rarely seen round the Border TV offices. Dressed in a velvet smoking jacket and chain-smoking Rothmans in an ivory cigarette holder, he would travel by chauffeured car from his rented castle, creep into the building up a private staircase, and lock himself in his bunker at the far end of the first floor. From there he would communicate with the staff almost exclusively by memo. People management was not his strong suit, but apparently he did manage to persuade his perched reporter that it would be a shame if she missed the dénouement of her unfolding soap opera in the *Daily Telegraph*.

That afternoon I was summoned to James Bredin's inner sanctum.

'Come.'

He stood with his back to me by the window, looking out over the rooftops of the Harraby council estate. Apart from the wraith of cigarette smoke he was perfectly still.

'Ayric . . .' That's always how he pronounced my name. 'Ayric, I've decided to offer you the job of reporter on one condition – that you don't smirk.'

Later, when people asked me how I ended up with a career in broadcasting, I always used to tell them it was because I didn't smirk. But as the Managing Director was still looking out of the window when Ayric left the room, he would never know, would he?

Back in the corridor I cheered and danced a little jig with Sylvia and Maureen. Harry Leyland and Charlie Weeds slapped me on the back and said they knew it had only been a matter of time till James Bredin saw sense. If he was listening on the other side of the door, he was probably regretting his decision already.

CHAPTER FOUR
THE CORRESPONDENT

The memo confirming my new job arrived the next day. A starting salary of £1,552 a year plus a special allowance of £100 per annum in lieu of overtime. Because of my lack of journalistic experience I would be given extensive training, and Mr Bredin would be grateful if I'd consider shaving off my beard. He also cautioned me about the particular danger of smiling too much when presenting programmes – a fault to which he feared I might succumb.

The extensive training happened the following Tuesday when an easy-going reporter called Lawrie Quayle from the Isle of Man came with me to cover a news story at Melmerby in the foothills of the Pennines. To make best use of the time, he gave me a driving lesson on the way. Children from the local school in Melmerby had built a refugee shanty town on the village green to give them a better idea of how poor people lived in distant lands. My suggestion that they could have been similarly instructed by taking a day trip to industrial Workington on the Cumberland coast was not well received. From what I remember, Lawrie went for a walk in the foothills of the Pennines while I pretended to know what I was doing. A week later I was a fully fledged programme presenter, the beard stayed, and – having made it into the big time – I just couldn't wipe the smile off my face.

In almost seven years I visited every nook and granny in the Border patch from Berwick to Stranraer, Peebles to Kendal. It's an odd region – the bit left over after all the other ITV companies had carved out their respective transmission areas. 650,000 people, four and a half million sheep, and a lack of hard news that could have been bottled and marketed as therapy. But what we lacked in armed robbery and serial killings, we made up for with really interesting stories. There was the chap who discovered a spaceman had appeared in the background of a picture he'd taken of his daughter, and the woman from Selkirk who was better than Albert Finney at impersonating Winston Churchill so long as she took out her false teeth, not to mention the noble Lord from Cumberland who'd been made an honorary member of the Bulgarian police force. Needless to say, *Border News and Lookaround* was (and still is) the most watched local magazine programme in Britain. We knew our patch and what the people in it wanted to see.

Sometimes I made the news as well as reporting it. One particularly frosty morning my drive to work was curtailed half a mile from the studios when my ancient Humber motor car decided to escape through the railings of a bridge. We flew and, sixty feet down, made a less than textbook landing, eventually crashing into one of the bridge supports. Miraculously, I walked out of it and was wandering about rather aimlessly when the crowds started to gather. A woman in curlers, craning to catch a glimpse of the mangled remains in the car, complimented me on getting to the scene before the police and the fire brigade. Later, while Ken De Vonald, the news editor, was showing me the seven hastily downed pints of lager cure for shock (he used the same cure each lunchtime to overcome boredom), he thanked me for being so considerate as to crash on a particularly thin news day. Scores of viewers rang to wish me well.

Because we were 'family' in a strange sort of way, we also gave occasional insights that the national broadcasters missed. Michael Jopling was a case in point. The honourable Member for Westmorland was well known as a particularly hard-nosed Tory Whip. Patrician, dour and unapproachable, it was he who once described Michael Heseltine as the sort of man who bought his own furniture. But when I interviewed him for some obligatory political quota programme – and because the programme was on Border Television, it wouldn't be seen in London political circles – he was much more interested in talking about his motorcycling experiences (which few of his bones had survived intact) and the fact that he stored Damien Hirst's sawn-up calves in formaldehyde in the barn at his house. The interview added little to the sum of knowledge about the workings of the parliamentary system, but it was certainly a jollier half-hour than we (and the audience) had expected.

When news stories did occasionally break, we pulled out all the stops, and despite the fact that Border was then the smallest mainland television station in Europe, we had reporters who could cover them with consummate style and professionalism. There was David Rose, who eventually went to ITN via BBC Scotland, where he once presented a programme called *Saturday Roundabout Sunday*. This was so dreadful it was universally known in the trade as 'The Tragic Roundabout'. We've all had one or two of those that we tend not to mention. Another colleague was Bill Hamilton, whose passions were railways and being a Football Association referee, so he naturally became the BBC's correspondent in Albania. And there was Michael Rodd, who moved on to *Tomorrow's World* but always remembered with great fondness his early days at Border, when he used to pad out the news programme by accompanying himself on the guitar while singing a topical calypso.

I got to ITN before David Rose because, for a time, I was ITN's Isle of Man correspondent. We're not talking James Cameron here, you understand. The title meant precisely nothing because, from one year's end to the next, precisely nothing that could be classed as news happened on the Isle of Man. The job did, however, mean that three times a year I would spend a week on the island with a film crew gathering reports on the state of the kipper industry, previews of the TT races, and stories about whether or not there really were fairies at Fairy Bridge.

Unburdened by news, our trips to the Isle of Man abounded with juvenile prank and adolescent excess. The fun would start in the bar of the Isle of Man Steam Packet Company ferry out of Heysham. The Irish Sea was invariably rough and breaking over the bows. The bar on the aged and creaking *Ben McCrea* had been cleverly designed with picture windows at deck level to give the impression that you were drinking in an aquarium during an earthquake. Ten minutes into the trip the director, occasionally a lady called Anna K. Moore, whose principal claim to fame was that she once did a variety act which involved tap dancing on a xylophone (perfect training for film direction), would report sick and disappear into a corner. That would be more or less the last we saw of her for the week. Once on the island she'd lock herself in her room and get her PA, Thirlie Grundy, to organise a shuttle service between the hotel and the chemists.

Neither I nor the cameraman, Eric Scott-Parker, was a good sailor, so much drink was taken in an attempt to match our equilibrium to that of the ship. Things weren't helped by the contribution of the captain, who invited us to stagger unsteadily to the bridge and cheerily told us that he was about to order the helmsman to be strapped to the wheel. With the wind in the direction it was, he would probably have to beach the ferry on the west coast of the island, he said, because any attempt to get into Douglas Harbour would result in us ending half-way up Victoria Street.

Cliff Goddard, the sound recordist, was a good sailor and, like all good sailors, smug with it. Eric and I drank and plotted. The weather having moderated enough to allow us into Douglas, albeit rather ungracefully, Dave Forsyth, the electrician, was despatched to the car deck to switch the plug leads on the film car that Cliff had chosen as his preferred mode of transport. Eric and I were poured into the equipment van, which Dave drove at some speed to the hotel. Twenty minutes later, Cliff kangarooed to a halt in the car park muttering about bloody Volvos and inadequate maintenance. Tomorrow he would drive the other vehicle whatever we said. We cheerily agreed and, as Cliff checked in, Dave corrected the plug leads on the Volvo and switched them on the van. By the end of the week, Cliff was incandescent and the plug leads on both vehicles were dizzy.

The Victoria Hotel in Douglas would have passed muster in Ceausescu's Bucharest. On the ground floor was a white-tiled drinking den from which any remaining customers were hosed out each morning. The smell of disinfectant spread to every corner of the building. The residents' quarters on the two floors above were guarded by a fearsome babushka who knitted constantly and believed that all men who stayed in the hotel were obviously perverts intent on deflowering any virgin they could smuggle past her glass booth. Given that about 80 per cent of the seasonal female population of Douglas appeared to be from Glaswegian hen parties intent on rape, pillage and the chemical removal of all unnecessary brain cells, that would have been a tall order.

The next day we put ourselves to work interviewing anyone who strayed close to the camera. On this trip we had to get our quota of stories in the can early because later in the week there was going to be a royal visit. This was my first experience of a form of professional aggravation that was going to become part of my stock-in-trade for some years. Royal visits, rather like moving house, show people at their very worst. Perfectly decent minor officials who normally can't do enough to help the boys from the telly suddenly adopt an air of Stalinist paranoia. Even though they've known you on first name terms for years and you were drinking with them in the bar of the Palace Casino the night before, they still double check your application for a royal press pass as if they've just discovered you're a fully paid-up member of the Red Brigades. Then there's the juggling for position on the various royal rota parties.

'You can't have your camera on the quayside when the Queen gets off the launch from the royal yacht because the BBC wants to be there.'

'And what's the BBC got that we haven't?'

'A camera position on the quayside.'

After four hours of walking the royal route, a fragile truce has broken out. I've managed to get a quayside camera position because I'm covering the visit for ITN as well as Border. The trade-off is that the car we've booked to take our film to the airport has to take the BBC's film, too. I ring the newsdesk at ITN to find out if they want anything for the morning bulletins.

'Shots of *Britannia* lying off Douglas will do.'

'I don't think you'll get that because of Mannanan's cloak.'

'And what the hell is Mannanan's cloak when it's out of the wardrobe?'

At a rush. 'Well, it's nonsense really, but Mannanan is supposedly the king of the Isle of Man who lives on Snaefell, and because he's jealous of other royalty he throws down a cloak of mist from the mountain that obscures them if they visit the island. It happened when Queen Victoria came here, and locals are saying it's probably going to happen this time as well.'

There's an ominous silence on the line from London followed by an enquiry about whether or not I'd been taking strong drink. The cloak of mist drifted down from Snaefell at seven o'clock in the evening. *Britannia* arrived at eight.

The call of salvation came at half-past nine from a fish merchant on the other side of the island. That afternoon, for the first time in twenty-five years, a sturgeon – the royal fish – had been caught in Manx waters. Did I want to film it? The cameraman was despatched, but it took me half an hour to pluck up the courage to ring the ITN newsdesk.

'Great. Get the film out on the first flight in the morning. Nice job, Eric.'

ITN's Isle of Man correspondent glowed.

'And it's certainly better than all that bollocks about cloaks and kings living on mountains . . .'

As I walked back along Douglas promenade towards Babushka's lair, I looked out to sea. *Britannia* might have moored in the Gulf of Mexico for all I could see of it through the cloak of mist.

CHAPTER FIVE
BREAKING OUT

By the time I got round to having a run-in with Prince Philip I was an old hand at royal visits, having done two of them – the Queen's foggy visit to the Isle of Man and Princess Anne opening a teabag factory in the Scottish Borders. Prince Philip had come to the Eden Valley to take part in the Lowther Horse Driving Trials, which involved four-in-hand teams of horses pulling gleaming carriages round a tough course through Lowther Great Park. The event was billed as the prince versus the scrap merchant, the scrappy in question being George Bowman from Penrith. The national press was out in force, which meant that if things ran to form Border's royal reporter would be about fifty-seventh in the pecking order, with as much chance of getting an interview as an invitation to holiday at Sandringham.

It was a hot, humid day and Prince Philip was not in a good mood.

He was in a worse one by the time he'd turned his carriage over on a tricky bit of the course. He walked back looking about as sulky as a Formula One driver who's just wrecked a million pounds' worth of car in a gravel trap. The press pack descended on him. He changed course, turned on his heel and walked straight into the Border cameraman, which gave me the chance I'd only dreamed of to ask the first, rushed question.

'How do you feel having had an accident that's put you out of the competition, sir?'

'How the bloody hell do you think I feel . . . stupid question.'

He glared, I blushed, and the crowd dutifully parted as he made to stride off.

Nerves, flustered embarrassment, bravado – I'm not sure what made me say it.

'It was a stupid question, sir, but manners cost nothing . . .' The last was said under my breath but obviously not far enough under my breath.

The words tailed away as he stopped in his tracks and ever so slowly turned. The assembled press were quieter than they'd been since the editor cut up rough about three bottles of claret on the lunchtime expenses. Amazingly, Prince Philip smiled.

'Quite right, too. Form an orderly queue and first the chap here who thinks his manners are better than mine.'

We got the interview, which for some reason sounded a bit breathless when we got it back to the cutting room, but almost more important was the comment later from one of the well-known national reporters.

'You lucky bastard. I thought he was going to have you for treason.'

Reporting for Border offered more variety than any job I've done since. Just filling half an hour a day was the challenge, and so the longer the idea the more gratefully it was received. I got my first chance to make documentaries. On a shoestring, of course. There was the story of the Blue Streak rocket, which was being developed in Cumberland and then shipped to French Guyana for test launches. The project was scrapped by the government to save money and the rocket flogged off to India as the basis of its fledgling space programme. And did we go to any of those places? Of course we did. Cumberland. A bleak stretch of moorland called Spadeadam Waste near

Carlisle where the rocket's engines had been tested and which was all of twelve miles from the Border studios. But we had a spot of luck that made the programme look grander than it really was. We managed to illustrate it with spectacular film footage of the test firings which we found in a rubbish skip on the site.

Nostalgia was cheap, too. We made a full programme about the memories of the projectionist at a cinema in Annan. The Gracie's Banking picture house had been opened by the government during the First World War to divert workers at the nearby munitions factory from their mission to drink themselves to death. The projectionist had been there since the silent era. When I asked him who his favourite screen actor had been in all that time, without hesitation he opted for George Arliss. 'But for some reason you don't see his films around much these days.' As he'd died in 1946 that was hardly surprising.

I bet you don't remember any of those programmes. I only do because they were my first, tentative steps. I could happily have worked as a reporter at Border TV for the rest of my days. Great patch, good friends and a small pool where it was relatively easy to swim as a big fish. Until at one drunken Christmas party Major Bennett, the office manager, told me to stop wasting the limited talents I had and that in his opinion I might even be able to get a proper job. Ambition began to fester.

The parting of the ways with Border came a few months later. Some obscure branch of the Home Office had invited television companies to devise a new sort of programme. Its aim would be to encourage viewers to do more voluntary work. I'd thought up a show called *Who Cares?* as the Border entry. We made a pilot and it won, beating entries from companies such as Anglia and Granada. The prize was £25,000 (a huge amount for a station with budgets as low as Border's) to be spent on producing the programme for national transmission and providing the necessary back-up to put potential volunteers in touch with organisations that needed their help.

We were celebrating Border's win in the production office – the bar of the Pinegrove Hotel – when the call came from James Bredin's secretary asking if I'd mind popping across to see him. This time Mr Bredin wasn't looking out of the window. Which was ominous.

'Ayric, sorry to drag you away from programme business . . .'

I try to work out the precise level of irony in the remark.

'Just wanted to congratulate you about *Who Cares?* . . .'

When he was nervous he used to flick his tie in a rather strange way.

'Unfortunately, I don't think it's the sort of programme we should be making, so . . .'

'You can't be serious.'

Faster flicking. 'I know you must be disappointed but it's my decision.'

'I am disappointed but more to the point, if you don't mind me saying so, I think it's a bloody stupid decision.'

I could perhaps have put that better.

'In fact, I've no option but to give you until four o'clock, and if you haven't seen sense and changed your mind I'm going to resign.'

At four o'clock he hadn't and I did.

The idea was taken up by Granada and became the long-running series *Reports Action*, but that didn't help me with the immediate problem of how I was going to tell my mother that all her efforts had been in vain because I'd packed in my job. I'd become a twenty-nine-year-old ex-broadcaster.

Perhaps I'd get drunk until a better idea occurred to me. Now, as chance would have it, British Nuclear Fuels, which was one of my favourite journalistic targets in those days, was having a press do in Carlisle that evening. A handful of canapés, enough drink to float Sellafield and, for decency's sake, a short PR chat about how BNFL was the best-run company in the universe. I set off to have a wake at the safe, efficient and caring nuclear industry's expense. At some point during the evening – somewhere on the road from canapé to oblivion – I bumped into John Bird, the News Editor of BBC Newcastle. He said it really was time I stopped wasting my limited talents and, who knows, I might even end up with a proper job.

'Such as?' grumped the has-been reporter, privately thinking that the last thing he needed on this particular evening was a smart arse.

'Such as working as a freelance for the BBC.'

'Well, I have actually been thinking of a move for a while.' (Skirting round the fact that 'a while' was actually five hours.)

'So when could you start?'

'How about Monday?'

People always say it must be a scary moment when you first decide to go freelance. It isn't if you have no choice.

CHAPTER SIX
BBC

That Monday morning I did the first of many hundreds of commutes to work across the Military Road from Carlisle to Newcastle, skirting Hadrian's Wall through a spectacular sunrise. On Friday I'd been an £11,000 a year staff reporter. Today I was a freelance with a contract that guaranteed me £3,500 a year whether I needed it or not. What I apparently lacked in financial prospects I made up for with thoughts of the Reithian excellence to come.

Instead I got a rush job covering a minor but very angry industrial dispute at a shipyard in Wallsend. Proper news. But I almost didn't get my first freelance story. A group of union heavies were refusing to let us in to film the meeting. A bit of pushing and abuse started. Attempting my very best impersonation of Sir Winston Churchill, I suggested that it was, without question, in the public interest for the British Broadcasting Corporation to be admitted. The impersonation lost something in the delivery, mainly because one of the union men had his fingers up my nose at the time. My protestations that I was a fully paid-up member of the National Union of Journalists – and therefore a brother in arms – cut no ice at all. But suddenly the crowd parted in the manner of the Red Sea, and when I looked back one chap was mopping blood from his face and another was clutching an eye about to go black. Arthur Nick, the cameraman, diminutive and in his sixties, had used the heavy Arriflex camera on his shoulder to particularly good effect. Accidentally, of course.

'Stick that in your rule book,' he muttered as he strolled purposefully into the thick of the meeting. On many occasions I discovered that Arthur, who had started in the business hand-cranking a camera for his dad at the opening of the Tyne Bridge, was not a man to meddle with, despite the fact that his real passion in life was a toy train set.

When the Wallsend item was edited, it ran two minutes and three seconds. The duty news editor suggested rather sourly that I'd fallen into the dark ways of freelancing with remarkable ease. We were paid by the minute or part thereof, and the old hands always made sure that their items strayed a couple of seconds over to earn themselves an extra few quid.

From the start there was serious competition to see who could liberate most of Aunty's money each month. Stuart Prebble, a smooth southern import, was particularly good at it, a talent that he took with him to *World in Action* and the ITV Network Centre before his instincts failed him and he accepted the Chief Executive's job at ITV Digital. Unfortunately, that was shortly before the banks showed it the red card when it couldn't pay its bill to the Football League. I'd always told him he should on no account have anything to do with football, for the very practical reason that each match ties you up for about three hours, by which time you could have recorded another two items.

My individual best performance in that much more important sporting fixture – the journalistic cash register stakes – was the day the shipbuilding industry was nationalised. The report I did that day was cut and recut twenty-three times, and went out on everything from Radio 1 to the Nigerian Broadcasting Corporation and the World Service. Needless to say, I've always been wholeheartedly in favour of shipbuilding nationalisation.

The reporters and presenters at the BBC seemed to be a rather grander bunch than my old colleagues at ITV. *Look North* was presented by Mike Neville, who had the looks of a juvenile lead, the status of a local superstar, and an easy-going wit that often brought the programme to a halt as reporters, guests and studio crew alike collapsed in helpless merriment. This talent was particularly useful on thin news days or when our ancient broadcasting equipment broke down, or on thin news days when we pretended it had. In one item we filmed together, inspired by a decision to list a Second World War pillbox in the Northumberland village of Mitford as a building of special architectural merit, Mike played the part of a soldier who didn't realise the war was over and was still in residence. I was supposed to be the sensible reporter, but spent the entire item rolling on the ground and gasping for breath as tears of laughter streamed down my face. Over the years we had so many requests for a rerun that the film had the distinction of being the most frequently shown item on British television, but I'm sure *Dad's Army* must have beaten that record since.

Jake Kelly was a distinguished reporter and less prone to kindergarten humour. He was a towering and rather dour man who nevertheless brought great amusement to the rest of us by his ability to screw a perk or a freebie out of every job he covered. At the end of a particularly lucrative week in which Jake had come back with a new Barbour jacket, twenty pounds of designer biscuits and a set of car seat covers, the duty news editor decided to give him a real challenge by sending him to do a story at a coffin factory in Annan. Slightly huffed that the junior riff-raff were running a book on the outcome, Jake refused to say if he'd managed to get one cheap and whether or not it had brass handles. He eventually landed the ultimate perk. Having covered innumerable stories about the problems of the nuclear industry in West Cumbria, he came back one day with the job of head of public relations for British Nuclear Fuels at Sellafield.

Everyone was passing through. Paul Corley en route to being Controller of Programmes at Carlton Television, Nicholas Owen on his way to becoming the ITN Royal Correspondent, Richard Madeley dashing to meet Judy on the sofa. (I used to tell people that I introduced Richard to Judy Finnigan at a party in Manchester when he was still a shy and handsome young reporter and she was married to a colleague of mine at Radio 4. Well, I was at the same party, I knew them both, and I don't think they'd met before.)

In the meantime we got on with the daily business of being the footsoldiers of the greatest broadcasting empire the world had known. At the morning news conference John Bird would hand out the cuttings. He took more cuttings than Alan Titchmarsh, scouring every local newspaper from the *Hexham Courant* to the *Keswick Reminder* in search of stories to delight our evening audience. We would groan on cuttings days. A chain-saw exhibition in Haltwhistle, a cow in Berwickshire that had just given birth to triplets, a man in Penrith who'd made a model of the Vatican out of milk bottle tops. The problem with believing newspaper cuttings is that some other reporter has already elaborated on a dodgy story.

One winter's morning when I couldn't get to Newcastle because snow had blocked the Tyne Gap, John rang me at home in Carlisle with his cuttings list. From the start his suggestions had a feel of desperation about them. The staff of the air traffic control relay station on Great Dun Fell had been snowed in for some days and were dangerously close to running out of food. A vet from Appleby had taken to skis to be able to get to his patients, and thirty people had been trapped by blizzards in a pub on Bowes Moor. I set off with the crew in my battered Land Rover to contact the victims and raise the siege.

As it turned out, they were all victims not of the weather but of sloppy journalism, and they were mightily hacked off. The manager at Great Dun Fell told me in no uncertain terms he had a Snowcat that would go over fifty-foot drifts, and would I please stop bothering him because his breakfast was getting cold. The vet from Appleby said he didn't know where the story had come from. All he'd been doing was a bit of practice before his skiing holiday, and it's a poor do if a chap can't practise his skiing without some jerk from the telly wanting to make it headline news. We couldn't find the telephone number of the pub, so headed off to brave the elements on the climb out to Bowes Moor. The road seemed remarkably clear. As we set off up the hill, a Mr Whippy ice cream van was coming in the opposite direction. I promise that's true. At the pub we found the dishevelled tail end of a local birthday party that had obviously been in full swing for a couple of days. Having joined it, I rang John and told him that if he wanted to fill that night's programme, he'd better dig out the junked item about the chain-saw exhibition in Haltwhistle. We'd see him the following day, hangover and snowstorms permitting, if he promised to put his bloody cuttings through the shredder.

The morning shift at BBC Newcastle often started at 5.30 because, in the days before local radio, the freelance reporters also presented the northern news on Radio 4 Long Wave. We'd all been issued with 'The Key', which gave us the power to switch ourselves in and out of the network. We thought of it as the broadcasting equivalent of having your finger on the nuclear button. Brian Redhead and John Timpson on the *Today* programme were supposed to give us the briefest of pauses at 6.25 and 7.25 to allow us to opt in. If they were in full flow with some subject that particularly interested them, they'd often forget. We'd have to sit in our little studio in Newcastle waiting to throw the switch that cut off some politician or other in his prime. We used to have a competition to think of the great sound bites that Newcastle listeners may have missed because we'd opted out half-way through them.

'Never in . . .' Winston Churchill.

'You turn . . .' Margaret Thatcher.

'I take pride in the words, *ich bin* . . .' John F. Kennedy.

The night before early morning radio shifts, I used to stay at the Royal Turk's Head Hotel three streets away from the studios. I had a suite, which sounds grander than it really was. In fact, it was in a semi-derelict wing of the hotel that didn't have a fire certificate, and I had to sign an indemnity that if I was burned to a crisp I wouldn't sue. It was the same suite used by the actress Violet Carson when she appeared at the Theatre Royal across the road, but I never found one of her hairnets or got a chance to tell her that there was a woman in Melrose who objected to her wearing it during the day.

On a number of occasions, generally after one of the parties that so enlivened those years, I slept in. At a time when it was widely believed that the BBC announcer wore a dinner jacket to read the news, listeners in Newcastle got a chance to see what he really looked like as they watched their tousled reporter in carpet slippers and dressing gown hurtling down New Bridge Street through the pigeons and fast food wrappers. Focused as I was on that imaginary clock ticking towards 06.25.00, the run to the studio passed in a flash – sometimes literally as I never wear pyjamas. But it was altogether more embarrassing having to stroll back to the hotel in carpet slippers and dressing gown at 7.40 when the streets were full of people heading for work. The cheery night porter at the Turk's Head would make matters worse by shouting over the heads of the bemused check-out queue, 'She's in room 43 this morning, sir.'

I'd settled into the easy-going routine of another newsroom and I was making a decent living. My nickname among the copy girls and production assistants was Ching Ching (to differentiate me from Stuart Prebble – Mini Ching – who didn't trouble the BBC cash register quite so much). Because news seemed to be the only bit of the BBC that wasn't being constantly reinvented, I saw no reason why I shouldn't be there for another thirty years. The organisers of the Haltwhistle chain-saw massacre would become old friends, and I would actually mean it when I told the man in Penrith I'd be back to see him when he'd finished his milk-bottle-top model of the Empire State Building.

But then I met John Mapplebeck and everything changed. It's hard to credit that any broadcaster could have a profound effect on your life, but John Mapplebeck was no ordinary broadcaster. His office was known as Studio Five – the seedy bar of the Portland pub next door to the BBC. He drank vast quantities of Holsten Pils but still talked sense. His knowledge of Labour history was unrivalled, his mistrust of Margaret Thatcher boundless. He saw the world though a prism of enquiry that generated raging or hilarious conversation in the pub and great programmes on the screen. Three days into the first project on which we worked together, he gave me the most comprehensive bollocking I've ever had from a producer. If I wanted to spend the rest of my life churning out facile rubbish, that was fine by him. If I thought I could write, I was wrong. He could find any number of ten-a-penny reporters who would apply themselves better than I did. I was idle and, worse, superficial. The word hung in the air.

My first reaction was to tell him where to insert the beer bottle. But I didn't. That long, silent moment when I blushed and bit my tongue and the old, bleary-eyed drinkers in the Portland went quiet in mid-racing tip was the start of almost twenty years of some of the most enjoyable and challenging work I've ever done.

John was a gentle maverick. He started as a reporter on local papers in Leeds before moving to the *Manchester Guardian*. He worked for the Music and Arts department of the BBC in London before mistakenly believing what the Corporation said about its commitment to regional broadcasting and moving to Newcastle. It was some years later that John discovered even if he'd stayed in London he would have had a problem getting promotion in the BBC. The reason was that he had a picture of a Christmas tree stamped on the cover of his personnel file, the sign that someone, somewhere thought he had dangerous communist sympathies. Like the Labour Party itself, John's radical philosophy actually owed more to Methodism than to Marx – apart, of course, from the Holsten Pils.

In our cramped first-floor studio in Newcastle, which had started life as a ward of the city's lying-in hospital, John brought scores of programmes into the world that explored, as he would put it, the warp and weft of regional life. No Birtian gobbledegook troubled us. No focus groups darkened our door. John found talent being wasted here and there, and would persuade the people who had it to come and work for him in Newcastle. Film directors like Bernard Hall and Dave Pritchard, always skint, frequently drunk, and yet still able to work a cinematographic magic on budgets which national directors wouldn't get out of bed for. Bernard Hall went on to be a nationally recognised documentary maker before dropping out and becoming a postman. Dave Pritchard rose to the challenge of touring the world with chef Keith Floyd while fighting with his presenter about who'd have the last glass out of the bottle. Neither Bernard nor Dave was as successful without John as they were with him, and that's probably true for me, too.

To be able to afford the film documentaries, John balanced the books by making low-budget studio programmes. That was my job. Sometimes two half-hour programmes a week on any subject that took our fancy – they worked because John had applied his idiosyncratic editorial intellect to them. This may seem unsurprising if you harbour the notion that all television programmes are properly thought out by dedicated professionals. Not a bit of it. Next time you see a screen credit for Executive Producer, remember that's often a person who, like you, is seeing the programme for the first time on air.

John's real passions were football and politics. Both let him down badly and for similar reasons. The heroes had gone. Jackie Milburn playing for Middlesbrough for twenty quid a week in the days when they say you could shout down any pit shaft in the North East of England and call up a First Division side. Ellen Wilkinson – Red Ellen – the fiery MP for Jarrow who took the suffering unemployed of a forgotten northern town and forced a careless Establishment to look them in the face. Gazza and William Hague just didn't pass muster somehow.

We were safe enough with football, apart from the fact that I knew as much about soccer as I know about quantum physics. (Although I understand that chaos theory plays a part in both.) That doesn't really matter for a jobbing broadcaster: someone who knows bugger all about an awful lot of things. Letting John loose on politics was an altogether riskier strategy with a Christmas tree decorating his file. But Jim Graham, the BBC manager in Newcastle (again passing through on his way to becoming Secretary of the BBC, Chairman of Border Television and head of the Prix Italia judges), backed a hunch, slipped John's leash and waited for the allegations of bias to roll in. When they duly arrived, it was from Labour MPs incensed that their divine right to rule in the North East could be questioned. Their fury knew no bounds when during the argy bargy it quickly became clear that John had forgotten more about

Labour's founding philosophy than they'd ever bothered to learn. The Tory Party, on the other hand, thought John was an OK sort of chap. He took them seriously. John's view was that they genuinely couldn't help but make a dog's breakfast of things. It was in their breeding.

Mind you, fearless journalists that we were, we used to take a rather softer line on Tory policies when faced with Neville Trotter's mother. Neville was the unmarried MP for the oddly Conservative enclave of Tynemouth. Six feet six with a shock of wiry hair and size fourteen brogues, he was a gentle giant. His mother wasn't. She used to come to the studios with him to make sure dear Neville wasn't unfairly treated by the beastly broadcasters. She was dumpy, tight-hatted and stony-faced. Les Dawson could have played the part of Mrs Trotter very well. After one late evening political debating programme in which Neville had, characteristically, come fourth out of three, we retired to hostility to find Mrs Trotter fingering her handbag.

'How dare you subject Neville to those uncouth persons!'

The word 'persons' carrying connotations of slime and decay as she pointed at the representatives of Labour and the Liberals.

'Mr Mapplebeck, I shall be reporting you to Conservative Central Office, won't you, Neville?'

Neville smiled in a resigned sort of way, and John attempted to get him off the hook by making the point that he thought the honourable Member for Tynemouth had done terribly well in the circumstances.

'Circumstances,' she growled with an ominous deliberation that would have done justice to Lady Bracknell. 'The circumstances, as you put it, are that you forced Neville to be subjected to abuse by these, these, these socialists.'

Mrs Trotter's handbag, whether by accident or design, swept a couple of glasses and a bowl of crisps from the table. We all instinctively ducked. With dark threats of reporting us to everyone from Lord Reith to John Logie Baird, she swept from the building with Neville clumping behind still trying to get her arms into her coat, a task made more difficult because she refused to let go of her trusty handbag.

'You should keep her off the sherry,' said the man from Labour, suddenly brave now that she'd gone.

'And you should just hope she doesn't stand against you at the next election,' said John, perspiring slightly. 'Because she'd probably bloody well win.'

The party didn't last long that night.

Most years we took our political programmes on the road to Blackpool and Brighton, Harrogate and Bournemouth to the three-ring circus of the party conferences. We'd assemble a panel of local MPs who'd brave each other's gatherings of party activists. It was on one of those tours that we first worked with a rather shy and self-effacing new MP who, remarkably, became Tony Blair.

Labour was having its annual bloodbath in Blackpool that year. Those were the days. Sorry, those were the days before the Millbank thought police turned the Labour Party conference into an event so interminably stage-managed that Margaret Thatcher would have felt at home there, and where you couldn't hear yourselves think for the bleeping of Pavlovian pagers.

As usual the town seemed to be bursting at the seams with overweight lady union reps who glowered rebellion and were unnecessarily rude to the waitresses. Labour MPs, relegated for the week to the unfamiliar role of servants of the people, generally tried to keep out of the way for fear of being pinned to a lamppost by some harridan brandishing a copy of composite 43 and demanding to know their precise position on lesbian rights in Guatemala or the pensions of dinner ladies in Lambeth.

(Blackpool was a great deal more civilised during Tory conferences, or so the prostitutes who teetered in from Manchester or Liverpool for the week always maintained.)

After our live programme from the salubrious surroundings of a studio thrown together out of scrap wood and second-hand curtains somewhere in a multi-storey car park near the Winter Gardens, we would escape the more intense Labour delegates by retiring to the Grapes pub. The Grapes was a no-go zone for the politically correct because it was frequented by gangs of blokes in search of a different kind of utopia. They were hoping to bump into visiting hen parties, come to Blackpool from the mill towns of industrial Lancashire and with whom they hoped to roost. To the boys on the prowl round the hen house, Clause 4 was what you got down the side of your face if you mistimed 'fancy a fuck then?' However unlikely it may seem that a female delegate could be mistaken for a member of a hen party out for a good time, a combination of fourteen pints of Exhibition and the Grapes' troglodytic lighting could have led to a nasty misunderstanding. The Labour women stayed away.

We settled into our corner. John went to get the drinks while the rest of us chatted about what a perceptive little programme we'd just made. Tony, the freshly elected Member for Sedgefield, wondered if he should have chipped in so much. The restless Ian Wrigglesworth, once Labour then SDP and then Liberal Democrat, said that it would be nice if new boys deferred a little more to their elders and betters. The gentle rebuke was spoken in a snootily patrician sort of way. He was presumably practising in case he should happen to find himself in the Conservative Party one day. Sitting nearest to the door was Michael Fallon, at the time the dry-as-dust Tory Member for Darlington. He always sat nearest to the door just in case he should happen to bump into one of his constituents.

Michael's political beliefs would have sat happily in the court of Vlad the Impaler. He espoused all the policies since abandoned by the Conservatives and many illiberal measures lately embraced by New Labour. But he did play a mean game of pool.

The chant started somewhere near the one-armed bandit.

'Fal . . . lon, Fal . . . lon, Fal . . . lon.'

Michael eyed up the door but it was too late. The lads from Darlington were already blocking the escape route. To Michael's palpable relief, they turned their attention to me.

'It's the woofter aff the telly . . . gizanautagraff.'

'Bugger off, boys, we've had a hard day and unlike you this is our first pint.'

They let their suspicions about shirt-lifting rest and set into John Mapplebeck.

'It's the mad professor.'

John rose to the occasion by sinking his burst sofa hairstyle deeper into the collar of a worn tweed jacket and carefully studying the specific gravity and brewing details on his bottle of Pils.

'And whee's the tailor's dummy then?'

Tony Blair's face was suddenly the colour of his tie and, saying nothing, he flashed a boyish grin that would one day greet soldiers in Afghanistan, Nelson Mandela in Downing Street, and disgruntled NHS patients in a thousand photo opportunities. Having found nobody worth wasting a punch on, the Darlington army slouched away into the night in search of a grab a granny party or, if all else failed, a fringe meeting about breast feeding for single mothers.

Tony said, 'Gosh.'

'You'll have to do better than that if you're going to get on,' said Ian Wrigglesworth, ignoring the fact that a slab of the electorate hadn't recognised him either.

At a party not so long ago, John Mapplebeck reminded me of another Wrigglesworth moment, this time at the Labour Party conference in Brighton the year after he'd defected from Labour to the shiny, new SDP. We took him as one of our squad of MPs into the lions' den. He got a surprisingly easy ride on the programme as I remember, and afterwards we washed up in a rather trendy Brighton cafe for dinner. The ascerbic Labour Member for Manchester Gorton, Gerald Kaufman, was at the next table. As Ian passed, Gerald looked up and said, 'Back so soon, Ian?' For some reason, Mr Wrigglesworth's sense of humour seemed to fail him.

CHAPTER SEVEN
GOING LIVE

We were making so many programmes then that, unlike Ian Wrigglesworth, I'd become a well-known face in Seaton Carew – even if it was a face which viewers couldn't instantly put a name to. The chap with the beard who did programmes on politics one minute, gardening the next – the arts on Thursdays, celebrity interviews on Tuesdays.

I ventured into distant regions of the BBC – Bristol, Plymouth. One Friday night I was presenting programmes for both of them. A green and furry environment programme for BBC Plymouth and an angry studio debate about racism in St Paul's for BBC Bristol. Half-way through the programmes, which were going out at exactly the same time, the Plymouth main transmitter went on the blink. What happens then is that, having lost its signal, the transmitter hunts for one nearby that will give it something else to transmit. It found Bristol. Audiences were suddenly switched from Robson talking about otters in some sedgy dale to Robson restraining a studio full of baying black Bristolians. It says something about the interest generated by most BBC regional programmes that nobody seemed to notice.

It all could have been a recipe for broadcasting schizophrenia or, worse, delusions of adequacy, but fortunately there were good friends and professional colleagues on hand to keep those conditions at bay. Our studio director in Newcastle at the time was Alan 'Slippers' Farrington, so-called because, firmly attached to his pipe and careless of his spreading waistline, he'd achieved middle age by the time he was twenty-two. He was so unflappable he could have snoozed through the attack on Pearl Harbour while still directing the outside broadcast coverage. During an interminable interview with a noted Scottish polemicist, Alan popped onto my earpiece to say, 'Hit me again. I can still hear the boring bastard.' It didn't make the programme any better, but it cheered up the presenter and the studio crew no end.

The presenter's earpiece is his lifeline to reality. However much he may be convincing himself that this interview is breaking the mould of broadcasting as we know it, there's always somebody on the other end of the wire to tell him the truth.

John Mapplebeck could be an earpiece challenge, particularly during afternoon recordings when he'd had a leisured lunch in the Portland. Taking his text from a question I'd asked or an article in that morning's *Guardian* newspaper, he'd spend the whole programme with his finger clamped on the talkback button expounding a political thesis and apparently unconcerned that it was a one-way conversation.

The studio camera crew is also a canny barometer of interviewing success. We once had to pause a recorded interview with the cellist Paul Tortelier because the snoring of the chap on camera two had become louder than Mr Tortelier's anecdotes about the life of Brahms. I apologised to the great man, who immediately put the bleary-eyed cameraman and myself at our ease by explaining that the audience at Carnegie Hall often snores, too.

Then there were the side bets. In preparation for what they feared would be dreary programmes, the crew used to nominate a word or phrase that I had to get into the recording somewhere: giant anteater in a debate about local government corruption; Pina Colada in an interview with a man from the Church Commissioners. I drew the line at masturbation during an interview with Barbara Castle, although she spent so long concentrating on her hairstyle and make-up that she probably wouldn't have noticed.

Most broadcasters suffer from a heady mixture of megalomania and paranoia. I'm no exception. We're constantly told that tens of thousands – if not millions – of people are hanging on our every word. It can't be good for us.

Dear Eric,
   Great news. This week we got an audience share of 37 per cent and a big percentage of ABC1s, and that was against *Home and Away*.
   Well done.
The Commissioning Editor

Now, any sensible person should be able to spot the flaw in that note. Should we be surprised that 37 per cent of intelligent people don't want to watch *Home and Away*? The weather map or the potter's wheel could surely get a similar audience if put head-to-head with a slab of anodyne, talentless rubbish where the only good performances come from the brassiere engineering and the barbecues. No matter. It fuels the megalomania. You can preen about that 37 per cent all week, until the next figures come in and show a drop to 36 per cent. Despair. A whole 1 per cent of the audience has abandoned you, preferring instead to watch the suntan lotion sink in.

Dear Eric,
   Disappointing figures. I've thought for some time that you've been using words that had a certain inaccessibility for the average viewer.
   Maybe we should talk.
The Commissioning Editor

You race through the big words you used in last week's programme and find that they're all smaller than inaccessibility. Paranoia bites.

Why we take these memos seriously is a mystery, given that they're coming from commissioning editors whose stock-in-trade is plagiarism. The system works like this. Somebody thinks of an idea that pulls a big if undiscerning audience – let's call it *The Neighbours from Hell*. Every other commissioning editor then tries to find a lookalike programme, until the poor mutt from Channel 5 ends up with *Goldfish from Hell* because they're the last of God's creatures to have the treatment. The upshot of it all is the mish-mash of drivel that's colonised so much of the TV schedules.

But I shouldn't complain. Bad management in broadcasting has helped me no end. A long association with the BBC Outside Broadcast department began as a result of bad planning rather than good judgement. A producer from OBs rang the Newcastle newsroom to see if Mike Neville could stand in at short notice as a commentator because they'd forgotten to book one. US President Jimmy Carter was to visit the city in a couple of days' time, and the BBC was going to broadcast the event live. Mike, master of the entertaining ad lib, declined the offer for the rather odd reason that the programme wouldn't be scripted. Clutching at straws, John Bird, the news editor, suggested that there was a young lad called Robson in the newsroom you've obviously never heard of but who's daft enough to try his hand at anything.

'You're right. Never heard of him, but beggars can't be choosers,' was apparently the gist of the reply.

The producer, Peter Massey, best known for producing *Mastermind* for many years, duly arrived the next morning. A jolly little bloke from the Isle of Man, he certainly didn't look like MENSA's best PR man or a big shot OB producer. Like most

Manxmen, he sounded rather as a turnip might if it could talk. But having swapped stories about the kipper industry and the existence of fairies at Fairy Bridge, I realised this was a man I could do business with.

I didn't feel quite so confident on programme day. Nerves jangling like the chimes on an ice cream van at the very thought of my first live national broadcast, I turned up outside Newcastle Civic Centre and was taken in hand by a stage manager as laid back as laudanum and shown to the commentary box. To be more precise, I was shown to where the commentary box would have been if they'd had time to build one. In a cramped space under a scaffolded camera tower there was a card table, monitor and microphone, and an umbrella in case it rained. We rehearsed a few opening shots, and I began to sound a bit less strangled.

'Three minutes to on air.'

That's when the problem started, or at least that's when they owned up to the fact that there was a problem. At the time of his Newcastle visit Jimmy Carter was – how shall I put it – not in the first flush of his presidential popularity. It had been some years since he'd last seen a cheering crowd, and the roads from Newcastle Airport were lined with them. The presidential cavalcade was ordered to drive more slowly.

'Thirty seconds to on air. No sign of the cars yet, I'm afraid.'

'*This is BBC 1. United States President Jimmy Carter is this morning visiting Newcastle Upon Tyne, and we go live now to our commentator at Newcastle Civic Centre, Eric Robson . . .*'

I stared catalepsy in the face and wished I was back at Pickfords. Somehow we managed to set the scene as planned, and then when we got to the bit where President Carter ought to have entered triumphantly from stage right, we began a forensic examination of the crowds, the streets nearby and the birds in the trees.

'Latest is he should be here in about twenty minutes,' chirruped the production assistant from the scanner.

Flags and coats of arms filled for a while. Geordie pride and folklore helped, but I wisely drew the line at a verse or two of 'Blaydon Races', tempting as it was at the time. The commentary swept from Jimmy Carter's background in peanut farming to the precarious state of his foreign policy in the Middle East, all of which gave poor Peter Massey considerable difficulty in finding suitable illustration – a stall selling KP nuts and the doner kebab house in Haymarket having been rejected, presumably because they weren't sufficiently picturesque.

By the time Jimmy Carter arrived forty minutes late, every known detail of the city's architectural, social and sporting history had been shared with our audience. In my mind's eye rose a model of the president struck through with hat pins which, to this day, I'm convinced played no small part in his forthcoming electoral defeat. Anyhow, he did his speech and I fell off the air a gibbering wreck.

I was summoned to the scanner where the then head of Outside Broadcasts, the one-time rugby international Cliff Morgan, was on the phone from London.

'What you think of that then, boyo?'

'Bloody terrifying.'

It's hard to dissemble when you're about to throw up over a million pounds' worth of electronics.

'Now, I don't want you getting any smart-arsed ideas that you're the new Richard Dimbleby, boyo, but if you're prepared to do maybe ten years' apprenticeship you might be some use one day.'

Resisting the temptation to say that I'd just done ten years' apprenticeship in the last hour, I agreed.

So it was that every so often for the next three or four years I sat on Tom Fleming's shoulder. Tom, tall and bearded, the great man of the Scottish theatre with a voice like Glayva poured on purple velvet, was extraordinarily patient with his sorcerer's apprentice. My job was to stand in for him if he fell down the stairs in Westminster Abbey or under a bus on the way to the Cenotaph. He did neither. So, for programme after programme I sat in the back of the box and silently mouthed a phantom commentary which was very different from the one that was going out live.

Then Brian Johnston retired from the telly to concentrate on *Test Match Special*. For a time he'd been the commentator on the Lord Mayor's Show, and the apprentice was about to get an OB of his own. Over lunch in the canteen in Kensington House – one of those faceless BBC buildings stuck up a back street in Shepherd's Bush – the producer John Vernon, who'd worked for OBs for so long that he looked and sounded rather like a member of the Royal Household, ran through the complexities of the broadcast and the labyrinthine protocols we'd have to observe if we were to keep the Great and the Good of the City of London happy. Brian waited for the producer to go to the loo and told me how I should really do it.

'Say something nice about one float in three, don't even attempt to identify the sundry aldermen and hangers-on because who cares apart from the aldermen's wives and the hangers-on, and be as scathing as you like about the London Underground train on a low loader because it always breaks down or gets stuck on a corner. Easy as that.'

He was right. For a couple of years it went swimmingly. The aldermen remained nameless, the only nasty letters were from aldermanic wives, and the Underground train broke down on cue.

Then Simon Betts took over as producer and decided to be innovative. Until then, all our cameras had been in one location somewhere behind St Paul's Cathedral, where we could watch the parade go by. Too, too boring. Simon would have them dotted along the processional route. The predictable result was that the Marks and Spencer float appeared seventeen times, we saw the aldermen so often they became like old friends and just had to be named, and we almost missed the Lord Mayor in the State Coach. Simon was moved to light duties, and my reward for preventing the broadcast being a total disaster was President Tito's funeral.

It began as another stand-by job while Tom Fleming did the proper broadcasting. He'd been despatched to Belgrade to commentate on the pictures being supplied by Yugoslav TV. At the last minute Phil Lewis, another Welshman who'd by then taken over as head of OBs, got cold feet. The pictures coming by satellite would be OK, but what if the landline commentary circuits failed? Much better to have Eric sitting in a presentation studio in London with a cup of coffee, a monitor and the *Observer's Book of Balkan Military Funerals*. I suggested it might be a good idea to have somebody from the Yugoslav section of the World Service sitting with me to add a fact or two – not that he'd be needed, of course.

He wasn't for the first one minute and forty-five seconds of the broadcast, at which point the commentary circuits duly failed and Tom Fleming was left commentating to a wall in Belgrade. For two and three-quarter hours a man with altogether too many Zs and Ws in his name and I sat in a grotty studio in London, valiantly attempting to make sense of the spectacle that unfolded on the TV screen before us. Except that 'unfolded' has too great a sense of urgency to accurately describe what we were watching. The funeral cortege was moving so slowly it looked like a satellite fault. And if you can tell the difference between one sombre Yugoslav general and another, you're a better man than I am.

We attempted to brighten up the porridge of state mourning

by speculating about the chaos into which Yugoslavia would inevitably slide having lost its strong man. We added a touch of local colour. At one point Wzzywzzxy interrupted to say that the coffin was now passing his mum's block of flats and that she was probably getting a better view than we were. She probably knew more about the subject than we did, too. Only half in jest, I asked if she was on phone and if she might be at home.

If the long march to the mausoleum was wearing for us, it was obviously much worse for the audience. When I got back to Newcastle the next day, Geoff Wonfor, the film editor, thanked me for giving him the best siesta he'd managed since a drunken afternoon on the beach at Whitley Bay some years earlier. The words prophet, honour and own country sprang to mind.

At the time I was working with Geoff on a film documentary called the *King of Mardale* which we were attempting to salvage from the skip. (Another popular misconception about broadcasting is that it's run like a well-oiled machine. Some of its steersmen may indeed be well oiled, but there's so much gravel grinding about in the mechanism it's a miracle we ever get anything on the air at all.) *King of Mardale* was the story of a Lakeland valley drowned to slake the thirst of customers of the Manchester Corporation Waterworks. In the long, hot summers of the late 1970s, the ruins of the lost village of Mardale Green appeared out of the water. John Martin, a director from Penrith who bore a striking resemblance to an Italian lottery ticket salesman, had started to make a film about the place but then had to skip the country to Ireland, apparently with inspectors of the Inland Revenue in hot pursuit. The film was eventually found in a drawer filed between John's tax demands and the unsavoury remnants of a cheese sandwich. Unfortunately, most of the sound tracks were missing. Geoff said he'd remake them in spare moments before we had to go to London to dub the soundtrack of the film in a few days' time. A couple of nights of partying across the sticky carpets of Newcastle's Birdcage Club and a poker school on the sleeper rather derailed the plan. When we met up in the Great Northern Hotel at King's Cross on dubbing day, Geoff was still marking up the dubbing sheets – a complicated code of overlapping coloured lines that represent sound fades and cuts.

We'd booked dubbing theatre Y at the BBC studios at Ealing, which had the grandest commentary recording cubicle I've ever seen – a full Edwardian cinema complete with ruched silk curtains and footlights. In these splendid surroundings regional producers usually got whichever dubbing mixer nobody else wanted, but that day Sod's law gave us Alan Dykes, who was acknowledged to be the best in the business.

He slowly looked through the sheets with their tally of seventy-two spot effects which were standing in for the missing sound tracks – everything from the sound of a 1920s Austin Ruby driving through Mardale Green to the screech of a golden eagle.

After a very long pause Geoff and I flinched as he spoke.

'I haven't done one of these since I last worked with Harold Lloyd,' he said as he smiled rather pityingly and reached for the phone to summon an extra couple of gram-spinners, fleet-fingered chaps who would play in the noises from sound-effects discs.

It went better than we could have hoped until, a couple of minutes before the end of the film, Alan Dykes stopped and looked puzzled. Apparently, there was a track shown on the dubbing sheets which he couldn't find on any of the play-in machines. Sweating, Geoff shuffled back and forth through the sheets trying to make sense of the mysterious orange line until Alan ran a fingertip across the page, dabbed it to his tongue and beamed. It was marmalade from the Great Northern breakfast.

Geoff gave up film editing shortly afterwards and became the director of choice for performers like U2, Jools Holland and Paul McCartney. He was bone idle, congenitally unreliable and never mastered the art of buying a packet of cigarettes, but a prodigious talent seemed to overcome those minor inadequacies. He's not so much of a hell raiser now and looks a bit like the older Howard Hughes, but when we meet – like pensioners in the bus shelter on the prom – we mistily remember the good old, wild old days.

Some years after he went on the music circuit, Geoff rang me up late one Tuesday night. He said I had to make sure I was free the following day to be in his latest production. And here's the ultimate Trivial Pursuit question that's guaranteed to stump anyone who's not read this book (which, of course, will be most of your friends). Who played the part of Lord Justice Melford Stephenson in *The Beatles Anthology*? Why, the outside broadcaster, of course. Whether or not they ever used it I don't know, because my contribution only ran for seven seconds and I forgot to watch.

Geoff was married to and devotedly in love with Andrea, who for many years was the most powerful woman in British broadcasting. They met when she was working for Tyne Tees Television and Geoff and I were grubbing about at the BBC in Newcastle. Eventually she became head of programmes or some such at Granada, and continued to be inventive and creatively impressive through many years of cancer treatment. For her part she treated chemotherapy with the contempt it deserves.

But in earlier, happier days I used to be their lodger when I wasn't staying at the Turk's Head. It was during those times that I learned the skills needed to have breakfast in a war zone which I would find useful some years later.

Andrea: 'Morning.'

Geoff: 'There's no loo roll again.'

Andrea: 'At least there's bread this morning.'

Geoff: 'I find my fingers go through the bread.'

A matter of moments later from somewhere behind my left shoulder came a frying pan that hit the wall leaving a pretty pattern of fried egg and tomato.

Eric: 'Going far today?'

Andrea: 'London at lunchtime.'

Geoff: 'And the supermarket.'

Eric: 'Surely it's your turn.'

Geoff: 'OK, you go to the supermarket. And make sure you buy wholemeal bread. It may not be as smooth as Andrex, but it holds together better than white.'

Geoff often got his comeuppance. One night at a particularly heavy session in the Birdcage Club, Geoff refused to go home. I left him to it. When eventually he arrived back, Andrea and I were playing Scrabble. He'd lost his keys (again) and she refused to let him in. For some time he shouted and begged through the letterbox. Andrea shouted back, telling him there were some old blankets in the garage that he was welcome to use. Next morning Geoff was rather stiff, considerably hungover and even more chastened. His mood wasn't helped when he grumbled to the assembled newsroom about his best mate being the sort of bastard who locked him out of his own house. Instead of the sympathy he expected, I got a round of applause. Of such moments are great friendships made.

And I did sometimes help Geoff out – apart from keeping him in cigarettes for nigh on twenty-five years. One night in the BBC Club in Newcastle there had been a bit of a party to celebrate the arrival in the Port of Tyne of some warship or other which had connections with the mother of broadcasters. Geoff hit the navy rum with a vengeance and disappeared at some point during the proceedings. At the end of the night I stayed back to see Irene, the club steward, to her taxi. We were just about to switch off the club lights when we heard a vague moaning at the bar. Or to be more precise from the gents' loo. Locked in one of the cubicles and, as it transpired, in an embrace with the toilet pan was the gibbering Geoff. The toilet seat had fallen over his neck, and every time he tried to get up the ring of black plastic pushed him down again. He was in a bit of a mess when I liberated him, even worse by the time he got home and Andrea had scrubbed him down with the coarsest brush she could lay hands on. But the next morning he bounced into work without a care in the world, and entertained the assembled newsroom with tales not of malevolent loo seats but of being held captive by a stoker, who was seven foot three if he was an inch and who had designs on his body. Dave, the other film editor, who was partial to the occasional stoker, said rather acidly that there was no justice. And seeing Geoff looking far healthier than he deserved to be, I tended to agree.

CHAPTER EIGHT
DOWN TO BRASS TACKS

The phone call from David Filkin came out of the blue.

'I'm making a new BBC 2 network current affairs series in Manchester called *Brass Tacks* and wondered if you'd be interested . . .'

'Yes.'

'. . . in being one of the reporters.'

'Yes.'

'Well, as you don't seem too sure, you'd better come to Manchester to talk about it.'

The team I was going to work with for the next seven or eight years seemed to have been assembled from every outpost of the BBC. A bunch of broadcasting asylum seekers brought together in the Milton Keynesian New Broadcasting House in Manchester where we were going to do nothing less than change the face of current affairs television. That's what we told ourselves, anyway.

Our first live programme didn't so much break the mould as clog the plumbing. In the biggest BBC studio in Manchester had been constructed a black-draped, Kafkaesque set with interrogation areas and banks of apparatchiks manning the telephones. Cameras swooped on jibs and dollies out of the darkness and disappeared from whence they came. In this bleak setting we attempted to argue the case that the Moors murderer Myra Hyndley was a reformed character and should be released from prison. The late Lord Longford testified to her Christian conversion. The mother of one of the victims testified to the efficacy of hanging. It was not an edifying spectacle. The presenter Brian Trueman, who's a decent and intelligent man, tried to paper over the crass. Mike Dornan, the other reporter, and I positively twinkled with expectation. We brought a smuggled message from Hyndley in prison saying she was misunderstood, and we fielded calls from viewers, including one from a nun ringing from a telephone box who stretched Christian charity to its limits in her comments about Lord Longford.

We got pages and pages of newspaper coverage, and the programme was rightly panned:

'Brian Trueman looked as if he'd been cast adrift in an aircraft hangar.'

'Eric Robson and Mike Dornan reacted like naughty schoolboys caught with a dirty magazine in class.'

'The viewers' responses demonstrated what a truly dreadful place Britain has become, and the production values plumbed the gutter to new depths.'

True. All true.

But despite the best efforts of the critics, *Brass Tacks* survived and prospered thanks to its patron – Saint Brian of Wenham, as one of my colleagues described him at the time, grateful for having kept his job. Brian Wenham was the astute Controller of BBC 2. He was also the man who brought wall-to-wall snooker to the BBC. Among his pet hates were the airs and graces of the London Current Affairs departments. Having been used to a monopoly of current affairs production, they would tell him what programmes they were prepared to make for him. *Brass Tacks* in Manchester gave him leverage. He could tell his London producers what to do with series he'd wanted shot of for years such as *Man Alive*.

Brian and I sometimes had an abrasive relationship. Having given me a job on his network, he objected that I carried on with regional broadcasting. I obviously wasn't taking the job seriously. Playing at it. What made me think I could flit between Manchester and Newcastle avoiding the shitty end of the business which other people had to put up with? The excremental programme in question was the new Breakfast TV. He said that if I was prepared to do eighteen months of porridge – up at four and beaming on a sofa for two hours a day – he could more or less guarantee I'd end up presenting *Panorama*. It had been a long and liquid dinner after a rather better *Brass Tacks* transmission, and I told him if that was the trade-off he could stick *Panorama*. Roger Laughton, the new *Brass Tacks* editor, summoned diplomacy from the dregs of his wine glass and did his best to disguise the embarrassing moment by saying he thought I was an idiot. For some reason, I've never been asked to do *Panorama*, but at least the only sofa shift I've had to do was at Pickfords.

Ironically, it was while doing the very worst of regional television that I'd first met Roger Laughton. Somebody had come up with the idea of staging a BBC regional leek growing challenge. The allotment holders of Birmingham would take on the leek experts of the North East. Roger came from the Midlands, and I championed the champions in Ashington. It was a project that offered boundless opportunity for cliché and condescension. Flat caps and mufflers, whippets and funny accents. We duly obliged, and Roger and I never mentioned that first broadcasting partnership during all the years we worked together on *Brass Tacks*.

By the time he took over *Brass Tacks*, Roger was considered a high flier and was widely tipped to be a future BBC channel controller. In fact, he turned right rather than left and became head of the ITV Meridian company. Gruff and affable, sensitive and ambitious, he was going to turn *Brass Tacks* into a radical, campaigning programme, the TV equivalent of the *Guardian* newspaper. It was a tall order and we never achieved it, but the programme's unique (and expensive) combination of film documentary, studio debate and live outside broadcast did give powerful voice to the concerns of ordinary people who, for once, were offered the opportunity to take on bureaucracy or tormentor on equal terms.

Battered wives agreed to speak from a secret, secure house in Moss Side. Their softly spoken contributions were in stark contrast to the blusterings of arrogant husbands, who still clung to a belief that they had the right to 'keep order in their own house', as they put it. Manchester prostitutes eloquently dissected the moral rearmament lectures of 'God's Copper', James Anderton, Chief Constable of Manchester, who had made clearing the streets of hookers rather than drug pushers his priority. Parents and children in the hall of a tiny school at Uldale on the fringe of the Lake District marshalled an argument that left the educational bureaucrats who were trying to close their school with a D minus. At the time of the Cod Wars, fishermen on the deck of a sidewinder trawler in Hull fish dock argued for their survival with the roaring passion of deep water. Water into which they would cheerily have tossed the architects of the Common Fisheries Policy had they not been safely in the studio. Another contributor to that programme was the fishermen's MP, John Prescott. He turned up on deck wearing an extraordinary coat with an astrakhan collar that made him look rather like a central European arms dealer. The body language of the fishermen, who tried to sit as far away from him as possible (difficult to do on the deck of a sidewinder), said more about the honourable Member for Hull Fish Quay than any cheap gibes about his Jags and houses ever could.

We continued to have some glorious failures, too. Against the advice of the entire team, Roger insisted on going ahead with a programme about dog shit on Britain's beaches. We suspected it was an idea close to the heart of the programme's senior editor: Mrs Laughton. The researcher Sid Waddell, who later achieved fame as the Geordie darts commentator who reinvented the English language in alien form, dutifully rounded up a pack of dog owners to sit in deck chairs on Bournemouth beach. The scientists with their dark warnings of an epidemic of child blindness caused by Toxicara canis were in the studio reeking gently of formalin. Twenty minutes into a fifty-minute live programme, all questions had been asked and all arguments explored. The outside broadcaster was floundering but knew there was a man in the semi-circle of deck chairs who had a story which, if not funny, was at least long. The camera slowly panned left to where he was sitting – or to be more accurate, to the empty deck chair where he had been sitting until a moment ago. Into the empty frame leaned the head of the woman in the neighbouring chair. 'Ee's gone for a pee.' I don't remember much of the rest of the broadcast, but was told afterwards by the security man on the front desk that it was the funniest programme he'd seen in ages. Roger didn't join us for dinner that night. He was presumably discussing the finer points of television production with the senior editor.

On one occasion *Brass Tacks* achieved what was widely thought of as the Holy Grail for BBC broadcasters. A programme about factory farming was featured on the front cover of *Radio Times*. Unfortunately, our moment of glory was short-lived. The photograph was of a very pretty pink piglet with the banner headline: 'Should This Little Piggy Go To Market?' But what caused the hoo-ha was the mock government health warning underneath it:

Health Warning: Meat and Poultry May Seriously Affect Your Health.

The NFU was incandescent, there were questions in the House, the picture editor of *Radio Times* was sent on gardening leave. And to cap it all, a number of vets rang the magazine to say that the answer to the question on the cover was most certainly no, because the piglet looked as if it had swine vesicular disease and the whole herd of which it was part would most likely have to be put down.

Brass Tacks probably managed more good programmes than bad, but it did have one undisputed triumph. The PA on the series was called Annette Steinhilber, and she eventually became the first person to think this book is a daft idea.

Those years in Manchester provided a heady mix of hard work and harder play. Because most of us had been shipped in, we didn't have homes to go to. We spent our spare time either touring the restaurants of Manchester or working a round of parties.

One of the most memorable was Russell Harty's Christmas party. Russell was making his show in Manchester at the time, and Annette was working as PA on that series, too. Because of the constraints of production and editing, television Christmases are invariably in September or October. So it was that on a soaking wet autumn day the BBC outside broadcast unit turned up at Russell's house in Giggleswick, which had been suitably jollified with Christmas decorations. Ken Stephinson, the producer, feared that the programme guests – among them Cilla Black and Madge from *Coronation Street* – might find it hard to get in the Christmas spirit, so despatched his specially recruited professional bartenders, Sid Waddell and me, to lay in supplies from the local pub. We did our job so well that by the time Ken was ready to record, the party was in full swing and Christmas spirit was in overdrive. Nobody was at all interested in spoiling the fun by making a programme. Ken asked the floor manager to tell us that we should calm the buggers down. Easier said than done, as we'd entirely forgotten to add bromide to the pub order. For an hour glasses were replenished with tonic water. The party started to go off the boil. 'Get them to look as if they're enjoying it,' was Ken's next relayed instruction. Large measures for half an hour. This 'now you drink it, now you don't' regime carried on for the rest of the evening, with Sid and me fine-tuning the ho, ho, ho. The programme was supposed to end with the guests going outside to listen to the local carol singers on the lawn. Half an hour before they were due to arrive, the heavens opened. There were murmurings of dissent. But Sid and I were a match for them. Trebles all round got our Christmas partygoers to a state where they not only didn't mind the rain, they didn't even notice it. But I suspect there were some nasty Boxing Day hangovers that eleventh of October.

My billet in Manchester was in the genteelly faded surroundings of Mayfair Mansions. I shared a flat there with the occupant of a pair of jeans so tight and worn threadbare in the appropriate places they were apparently capable of driving even lady members of the Fabian Society to distraction. The socialist sex symbol in question was Michael Wood, who, for the first time since the days of Sir Mortimer Wheeler, managed to make archaeology sexy. His programmes *In Search of the Dark Ages* and *The Trojan Wars* may have raised the odd dusty academic eyebrow, but they made holes in the ground the place to be. The flat in Mayfair Mansions (which had been the Italian Economic Consulate in its glory days) took on the air of a book-lined gentleman's club. On a table in the huge and sunny bay window would be spread maps and research notes. Mike and I would track King Athelstan through the kippers, Heinrich Schliemann round the marmalade jars. They were perfect mornings in which we'd slowly recover from the excesses of the party of the night before. Mayfair Mansions had become the *Brass Tacks* hospitality suite. Our proud boast was that we had sufficient crockery and cutlery in the flat to cater for 150, and Mike's good looks and good company ensured that volunteer dishwashers were always in plentiful supply. Some of them even espoused feminism when they returned to the office after a lengthy Fairy Liquid shift.

I should say that one of the reasons these times in Manchester have retained their sparkling memory is that the other end of my life was falling apart at about the same time. I was married with two small children, Julian and Charlotte, but the marriage had been faltering for some time. Manchester provided a bolthole.

At about that time Roger Laughton was plotting the expansion of his Manchester empire. It was during a conversation at Mayfair Mansions that he first proposed a series called *Great Railway Journeys of the World*. It wasn't a series for train buffs. It had nothing whatsoever to do with the lonely figures standing on the end of a platform at Crewe marking down the numbers of passing coaches. This was going to be a series of railway adventures where the trains were the time machines that took us into other peoples' worlds. Mike was to be one of the travellers. I wasn't. Roger wanted big names, and the outside broadcaster's wasn't anywhere near big enough. With commendable honesty, he sat in Mayfair Mansions, drank my coffee and told me so in just those words.

He got his cast list. Michael Wood was joined by Michael Frayn, Ludovic Kennedy, Miles Kington, Michael Palin, the playwright and novelist Brian Thompson, and Bill Grundy.

Four months later, Roger was back at Mayfair Mansions, slightly less confident and blunt this time, because he was trying to think of a rather more diplomatic way of asking me if I'd do him a great favour by getting him out of a hole. Bill Grundy, who'd been the traveller on the European journey, had apparently fallen down the neck of a whisky bottle in Zurich and been air-freighted home.

'I know I've a cheek to ask, having turned you down originally, and I'd quite understand if you told me to piss off, but as you're nothing if not professional –' (Well, I suppose that's one step up from being just nothing.) 'I'm sure you'll consider the request in the spirit in which it's . . .'

He tailed off.

'No problem. When do I start?'

'Well, there is a problem, actually.'

Roger could always spot a soft touch, and having seen enthusiasm in my eyes, he was instantly back on form.

'The film's already been shot and we can't afford to shoot it again, so you won't actually appear in it.'

As the series was supposed to be based on the conversations that would spring up between the various travellers and the people they met on their journey, that seemed quite a challenge.

'But we'll do a piece to camera with you at Victoria Station, and I assumed you were going to say yes, so I've booked you to do the whole journey on your own starting on Tuesday.'

On Tuesday I packed my bags and headed across Europe. Before I left, I looked at the rushes of a journey that would take me through France and Switzerland, Austria and Hungary, and on to the borders of Czechoslovakia. I watched the bits Bill Grundy had filmed before the bottleneck, thought I could have done them better and said so. Roger was in no position to do anything but agree, whatever he really thought.

As I packed I wondered how my attempt at a journey once removed would compare with the other programmes in the series. The answer was simple.

Badly. I was going to be putting my career as a documentary filmmaker in jeopardy just to avoid an embarrassing hole in Roger's series. But as I didn't have a career as a documentary filmmaker in the first place, where was the problem? The imagined point of principle evaporated, but not before I extracted from Roger a promise that if he got another series I would be allowed to do one of the programmes properly.

I've got to say it was a great fortnight's holiday at the BBC's expense. Tootling from train to train up hill and down dale and, even better, without the usual demanding film crew in tow. Time to do what *Great Railway Journeys* were all about – chatting to fellow travellers, exploring the branch lines of European history, and spotting the differences between what the crew had been allowed to film and what things are really like when the BBC isn't there with the official minders from the railway companies.

At the border crossing between Austria and Hungary at the Cold War outpost of Hegyeshalom, the rushes had shown the shunted arrival of a smart dining car complete with chintz curtains and tablecloths, flowers on the tables, and a menu and service that would have done justice to the Orient Express. The day I was there the dining car of the Hungarian state railways, Magyar Allamvasutak, was shunted on with such ferocity that one of my fellow passengers was bounced onto the floor. When the rattling stopped and I strolled along for breakfast, there wasn't a tablecloth or bunch of flowers to be found. The coal-fired kitchen was reeking fumes into the carriage, and a swarthy waiter-cum-chef with the most extraordinary bleached afro hairstyle was altogether more interested in selling me black market currency than the charred pork chops and rough bottled Pilsner that was the only breakfast on offer. It was one of the great sequences that viewers of *Great Railway Journeys* never saw.

Another was in the Hotel Gellert in Budapest. As part of the bribe to encourage me do the journey, I'd stuck out for the suite where Zaharoff, arms dealer to kings and revolutionaries in equal measure, had carried on his dodgy and immensely profitable business. I stepped out onto his balcony in a pink evening light, and looked out over the twin cities of Buda and Pest just as he must have done before signing a deal for a couple of shiploads of armaments that would reinforce Balkan instability for another few months. It was idyllic. He probably thought so, too. What a view; what a profit.

I went down to dinner. The hotel dining room where he would have entertained his bellicose clients was slightly bigger than Wembley Stadium, but the night I was there I was one of just two guests. We sat at tables so far apart that a telephone call between us would have been classed as long distance. Somewhere in the shadows there were the strains of a Czarda orchestra. During the foie gras they came closer. By the goulash they were in my ear.

'Where from you are come? Maybe God Bless America?'

The stomach straining the buttons on the gypsy waistcoat was leaning on my shoulder.

'Scotland.'

'Scootland is bravo, noh?'

I was treated to three versions of what may have been Scootland the Bravo (but equally it could have been anything from an attempt at Rogers and Hart to Czarda punk rock) before a fistful of local currency sent them on their long and jangling trek to the other end of the dining room. Enough time for dessert and to reflect again on what the *Great Railway Journeys* viewers weren't going to see before the band had a chance of getting back.

Next morning I wandered through hotel reception where my official minder was pretending to doze behind a newspaper just like in the movies. I told him I was going to the toilet.

'Toilet. Toilette. Toy Let.'

The mimed flushing chain and thumb and finger on the nose eventually got the message across.

I escaped out of the back door and headed for the Budapest equivalent of Barry Island. Because it was a scrapyard, the last resting place of generations of old-fashioned Eastern Bloc steam locomotives, and therefore not the image that modern Hungary wanted to promote, it was off-limits. From the city centre with its Coca-Cola neons and Levi's hoardings, I walked maybe a mile through suburban streets of increasingly dilapidated clapboard houses. The image of Hungary's dynamic new market economy unravelled in that twenty minutes. By the time I arrived at the yard, I was in impoverished Eastern Europe.

A friend of the train-spotting persuasion had told me to look for a gap in a wooden fence under an elder tree. It's amazing how, even in the days before the internet revolution, these little local details could find their way from a breaker's yard in Budapest to a railway enthusiast in Stockport.

But there it was. One fence, one elder tree and one anorak-sized hole between the vertical sleepers. I slipped in under cover of brambles and spent an hour happily snapping away at the redundant, rusting giants of communist main line steam. Until I felt a tap on the shoulder and almost expired on the spot. The stubby finger belonged to a peasant woman from central casting: grubby headsquare, acres of faded flowery print stretched across a gargantuan chest and bulging biceps. She boomed at me for some minutes, her prodding finger now whirling in angry semaphore.

I turned and ran, reasoning that she was obviously built for on the spot violence rather than speed. Brambled and sweating, I stumbled back into the hotel and was really rather pleased to see my fuming minder pacing about in reception. He was miffed not just because I'd done a runner – virtually all visiting journalists try to do that. No, that morning he had planned an educational excursion into the forests above Budapest to see the socialist ideal of railways at work.

The passengers on the gleaming red and yellow diesel train were adults, but the drivers and guards were all children. If they stuck in at school, as a reward they could spend their weekends on the Pioneer Railway. In the staff canteen, while they tucked into their bait of crisps and lemonade, they told me that if I came back to Hungary in a few years I'd be able to travel on trains from the space age that would take my breath away. It being a thoroughly bad idea to undermine the idealism of little children with wide eyes and sparkling smiles, I took another sip of over-sweetened lemonade and told them that of course they were absolutely right.

But I wasn't looking for the brave new world of railways. I'd travelled across Europe in pursuit of a retreating age of steam. As I wrote in my notebook at the time:

At every stop there are railwaymen who lean on booking office counters, shake their heads and tell stories of the trains that used to run and the steam engines that were here just the week before. Then suddenly, on a reservation up near the border with Czechoslovakia, there they are: dinosaurs grazing. Beasts from the mythology of railways that are still a potent reminder of past endeavours. No main line train is entrusted to these steam locomotives now. They'll shunt freight into a brief twilight and then be left to grow cold.

It will fall to the enginemen of Hungary to damp down the fires of European main line steam, but when they do, it will be with the same conflicting emotions as men of the breed in Doncaster or Crewe.

Not a dry valve in the house. It did me no end of good with the steam railway buffs, but then they're hardly renowned for their critical faculties. When the series went out, the other programmes attracted considerable critical acclaim. Mine, tacked on the end, basked in their reflected glory but was an unhappy compromise.

My own favourite programme in the series was the journey from Bombay to Cochin travelled by Brian Thompson. It was a great programme – heat, dust and steam. More importantly, in India just before filming, I tentatively suggested to Annette, who was the unit manager on the project, that we might consider getting married. She said yes in a half-hearted, embarrassed sort of way, and steamed off from Poona into the pink haze of an Indian evening checking her film schedule and cursing the Indian railway bureaucracy. She may just have been proposed to, but she also had a job to do. At that moment work was far more important. For my part I set off on a solitary journey home to Manchester.

The following year Roger Laughton got a commission to make a series called Great River Journeys. I set up camp in the reference section of the Manchester Central Library and began researching a trip up the Congo. I would arrive on the merchant ship *Fort Elizabeth*, rolling on a long swell. While still a day's sailing from the Congo estuaries, we'd be surrounded by the islands of vegetation that are washed more than eighty miles out to sea by the half-million cubic feet of water that the great river spews into the Atlantic each second. Beneath our hull would be the 4,000-foot-deep canyon that the Congo has carved into the ocean floor. Our river journey along the border between Zaire and Angola would take us almost 3,000 miles, to the village where Livingstone himself died.

Roger invited me to dinner at a restaurant in Didsbury to talk about the idea. We discussed the programmes we'd made together, how he relied on me as he relied on nobody else, and how grateful he was that I'd bailed him out on *Great Railway Journeys*. A 'But' was lurking behind the bottle of claret. Eventually, I interrupted the flannel to remind him of our deal.

He ratted on it.

'Sorry, you're just not well enough known.'

CHAPTER NINE
IN THE GOLDEN TRIANGLE

I made one mistake in that meeting with Roger. I was so angry I insisted on paying for my own dinner. And what sort of freelance is that? On the way home I told myself I obviously didn't deserve the job. Very soon I was telling myself I was too damned busy to be messing about in the Heart of Darkness for three months anyway. I got on with other things. At the time there was plenty of choice.

The BBC Outside Broadcast department had decided it was time I flew solo on a grade one OB. I'd practised on the Lord Mayor of London. Now they felt I was ready to be let loose on the Queen. John Vernon asked me to commentate on the State Opening of Parliament. I wouldn't have the broadcast to myself. The BBC's Political Editor, David Holmes, would do all the stuff inside the Palace of Westminster, but I'd have the ceremonial route from Buckingham Palace. Over the years I'd get to know that trot very well. In the business they call the wedge of central London bounded by Buckingham Palace, Trafalgar Square and the Houses of Parliament the golden triangle. So many of the great events of state happen within it that it's been hard-wired for pictures and sound with cabling in ducts under the roads. The outside broadcast units simply pull up and plug in. As ever, less thought had been given to where the poor commentator had to work. For the State Opening, David and I were crammed into the House of Lords post room. It wasn't comfortable, sandwiched as we were between piles of overheating electronics and the pigeonholes containing their Lordships' football pools. Outside it was a bitterly cold November morning. In the bowels of the Palace of Westminster David and I were dripping in a Gothic sauna.

But with the first glimpse of the Captain's Escort emerging from the central arch of Buckingham Palace, all thoughts of personal discomfort disappear. Outside broadcasts are a bobsleigh run. The time flies. The world speeds up – assuming, of course, that you're not waiting for President Carter. But the Queen is better at this sort of thing than any president. If the Irish State Coach is scheduled to come through the front gates of the palace at eleven o'clock and thirty seconds, you can more or less guarantee that it will. On the rare occasions when there's been a delay, I'm told the Queen has an inquest the moment she's back in the palace. Only problems involving horses or harness are acceptable excuses. Human error is assumed to have been abolished.

In fact, the timings are usually so precise that some commentators almost work to a script. In the forty-five seconds it takes the head of the procession to get from the royal salute at the gates of the palace to the far side of the Victoria Memorial, you can explain that the Irish State Coach, almost always used for the State Opening of Parliament, was built in Dublin in 1851 and bought by Queen Victoria. You might even have time to name the coachman and mention that he's in charge of two bay horses called Kestrel and St David. I never write any of this stuff down in a script, never use a card index as some commentators do. Instead, I usually get up at something like four o'clock on the morning of the broadcast and commit it all to memory.

And that's because of a recurring nightmare. President Carter is driving down the West Road in Newcastle in the Gold State

Coach – twenty-four feet long, thirteen feet high, built for the coronation of George III in 1761. It's covered with gold carving and upholstered in plush red velvet. Four tritons – mythical sea gods – support the carriage, and eight palm trees form the framework of the body and hold the roof in their branches. The president is wearing a tiara made for Queen Elizabeth the Queen Mother and a gown richly decorated with pearls and gold thread. In the palm of his hand and resting on a velvet cushion is a packet of peanuts. But just outside the Tyne Theatre a wheel falls off the carriage, and it takes the AA almost an hour to get it back on. And my script's too short. I run out of things to say.

So I always go into a broadcast with enough material to fill it three times over. The danger then is that the whole event runs like clockwork, but you still try to include all this fascinating, carefully researched material. If that's happening it's easy to spot. A commentator who starts out at a measured pace that befits the occasion gradually turns into the racing commentator Peter O'Sullivan in the final furlong. If you've got your extensive notes written down, there's also the problem that you spend more time with your eyes on the script than on the event that's unfolding in front of you.

Tom Fleming used to write a lot of his fine purple prose and was a master of the grandiloquent phrase. During one sombre event on a drenched London morning, he actually said, 'The very heavens weep.' Bit over the top for my taste, though I'm sure it brought a tear to the eye somewhere. There's a trade-off, however. The carefully prepared pithy or portentous phrase is fine, but if somebody has just run out of the crowd in the Mall and tried to climb aboard Princess Anne's carriage, and because you're reading your notes at the time you don't see it and therefore don't mention it, people at home – who *are* watching the pictures – tend to notice. They wonder if you're commentating on the same event that they're watching.

There are just three golden rules for the outside broadcast commentator:

1 Don't take your eyes off the monitors.
2 Use as little commentary as possible (most commentators are altogether too keen on the sound of their own voices).
3 Make sure that Helen Holmes is in the commentary box with you.

For many years Helen was the principal researcher for BBC outside broadcasts. She could be haughty, she could be difficult, but she had great contacts. She could wheedle out extraordinary facts and fancies that enlivened many of my commentaries. She also happened to be the sister-in-law of the man whose collection of armour was the subject of that very first programme in which I appeared modelling the rivets. Small world.

The State Opening went reasonably well, and I remember coming home on the train from London harbouring notions of being the voice of BBC events coverage. Of course, it didn't happen. I was given some big broadcasts – a two-hour Christmas Eve special celebrating the Queen's Silver Jubilee in 1977 was the biggest. But when it came to live OBs, Tom was still the man, and when Charles and Diana's wedding hove into view I was stand-by commentator again. The amount of preparation for that broadcast was enormous. Tom didn't break a leg on the morning of Wednesday, 29 July 1981, but I had to assume he would. I had to be able to tell the difference between the Lord Steward and the Lord Chamberlain, the Dowager Duchess of Abercorn and the Duchess of Grafton. I had to know which car contained the King and Queen of the Belgians and be able to differentiate between the Princess of

Liechtenstein and the Grand Duchess of Luxembourg. All easy in theory but more problematic when they're in a crowd. I think that rather as a sop I was also given the job of being the reporter on the wedding coverage. I appeared fleetingly on a balcony of St Paul's Cathedral and duly reported on the events that were unfolding below. But for most of the four-and-a-half hours of the broadcast, I twiddled my thumbs and occasionally checked that Tom Fleming's legs were still in one piece.

CHAPTER TEN
WINNERS AND LOSERS

What I lacked in broadcasting glory I made up for in glorious variety. It was a golden time when money was being spent on daring projects that weren't yet held hostage by the ratings wars and lowest common denominator decision-making that would come to dominate all the networks.

Mary Price, an uncompromising radio producer from BBC Bristol, asked me to go to Ireland for a few weeks to make an episode of a new Radio 4 series called *An Ever Closer Union*, which consisted of audio portraits of all the European member states. The series was certainly a high-risk strategy. The programmes were each up to ninety minutes long, and I suspect so bored even the discerning Radio 4 audience that they generated a deep and enduring suspicion of the great European project.

The only memory of the programme that endures with me is of Sunday lunch in a monstrous house in the bogs of Roscommon – home of one of the great Anglo-Irish families. The mansion was notable because it was the first in the world to be built of reinforced poured concrete. Time had not been kind to it, and the house, streaked and stained, looked as if it was suffering from some contagious disease. If this was the prototype, it's amazing the technology survived. Until shortly before we went there, the sole resident had been an ancient lady who camped out in a few decaying rooms without benefit of electricity. Her water supplies had to be brought by donkey cart from the nearby village. She had recently died – we assumed either frozen to death or drowned in one of the waterfalls that came in through the roof – and the place had been taken over by her nephew and his family. Now family loyalty and tradition are fine and dandy, but he'd given up a successful career as a Dublin merchant banker to come and live in this derelict concrete eyesore at the heart of a much diminished estate.

Mary Price wangled an invitation to lunch so that we could find out:

(a) what made the Anglo-Irish tick,
(b) if they still had any relevance in modern, European Ireland, and
(c) if they were barking mad.

By the time the roast beef was being served by the merchant banker's wife, who had a hooray Henrietta accent that Camilla Parker Bowles would have found impenetrable, we'd had a stab at the first two questions. We'd oohed and aahed at the family heirlooms, including a harp which had apparently belonged to the bard of a particular Irish king. We'd discussed the briar patch that is Irish politics. But with the gravy and horseradish sauce came the answer to (c). Suddenly the merchant banker and his two angelic, blonde-haired sons leapt to their feet, grabbed tennis rackets and started to shout 'BATS'. They then charged about the dining room lashing out at invisible aerial interlopers. After five minutes, no bat having been served but with innumerable footfaults over the furniture, the rackets were put aside and lunch continued. The conversation picked up where it had left off and no reference to the Wimbledon moment was made. The answer to (c) was resoundingly yes.

At times I would hanker for the lunacies of Roscommon in the months that followed. I'd traded rural Ireland for the square mile of neglect and decay that was the old East End of Glasgow, and the lunacies there were in a different league.

The series on inner city Glasgow was made by the Manchester Entertainment and Features department for BBC 2 in the face of considerable opposition from BBC Scotland, who thought the Sassenachs incapable of understanding the nuances of Glaswegian life.

On one level they were right. We were outsiders in an alien world. We struggled to understand how the Barrowfield estate, in the badlands out by the Celtic football ground, could be terrorised by two gangs of little kids. The Torch and The Sword fought pitched battles in its main street, known locally as Nightmare Alley, each night as darkness fell. It was harder still to understand the bravery of community bobby Kenny Ross, who stood between them, smiling at the daubed signs which declared that 'Ross is a poof', dodging the flying paving slabs, and talking the people throwing them to a standstill.

Was it a 'nuance' that some residents of Barrowfield had chopped up their own doors and floorboards for firewood and sold their hot water tank and plumbing for scrap? And I don't think 'nuance' adequately describes the picture of their grannies sitting in a pool of their own urine in the corner of the Mecca Bar by the Glasgow Cross, clutching a can of Carlsberg Special Brew and mouthing a few tuneless bars of 'Flowers of the Forest'.

There were moments during the Glasgow filming when I had to close my eyes tight shut for a few seconds to convince myself I was still in the same century, let alone the same United Kingdom. The afternoon we went to the bar at Glasgow Cross, we were allowed in only because we were with the local Salvation Army captain on his rounds. But we'd been in the place for barely ten minutes when one of the alcoholic regulars laid our escort out for having been refused a bed at the Salvation Army hostel the previous night for being drunk. At Paddy's Market there was an old lady trying to sell wire coat hangers. In an abandoned tenement there were a couple of drug addicts who hadn't eaten for six days. They lay on a dirty mattress in an otherwise bare room. The girl was expecting a baby the following week. Well, she thought it was the following week, but she'd rather lost track of time as well as sanity.

For a while we thought the series would be unacceptably bleak, that we were the wide-eyed incomers gawping at Glasgow's various despairs like tourists venturing out of an air-conditioned hotel in Port-au-Prince. Maybe there had been a grain of truth in what our colleagues at BBC Glasgow said after all. But we touched a raw nerve with the series. And even the Glasgow press thought we'd got it depressingly right:

> Discreet as an undertaker with the newly bereaved, Eric Robson moved round the blighted East End and talked to its people. Some clips were shown of the heyday of Red Clydeside – tanks on the streets and soldiers at every corner; it could have been film from another planet, so eerily remote did it seem.
>
> As Robson wound down his glum voice-over, Glasgow humour – which laughed off the Luftwaffe – was silent. There wasn't even an echo in the wasteland.

One of the people the glum undertaker talked to was Barney, a down-and-out alcoholic who was a compulsive painter. He produced detailed, imagined Glasgow cityscapes on scraps of hardboard rescued from skips and rubbish dumps. And at the centre of each of them was the beacon in his life – Barney's Bar. We helped him through the social services system into a flat of his own, and when we left I offered to buy one of his pictures.

He wouldn't take anything for it because he was a proud man and he owed me a favour. I still have a picture of Barney's Bar on my kitchen wall.

And there was Jimmy Grimes. I left Glasgow with Jimmy Grimes. He said he was one of the city's survivors. He played the system. He paid no tax, claimed no benefits and appeared on no official lists. Every time we met him he was at a different house. He was planning to sail from the industrial graveyard of the Clyde to paradise – perhaps even the Caribbean – on his fourth-hand sloop *Spirit of Freedom*. I said I'd go with him, at least as far as Dunoon. We set sail one Thursday morning. By lunchtime the sloop was taking in so much water we had to stop for repairs. We'd done about six miles. The tide was going out so we ended up high and dry on a mudbank in the middle of Dumbarton Harbour. We waded ashore and got gloriously drunk in a harbourside bar; we talked about the good old, bad old days and the boundless opportunities to come. Jimmy said that if I even thought of singing 'Glasgow Belongs To Me', he'd put my lights out.

CHAPTER ELEVEN
BEGG

I t was about this time that I met Begg. Michael was the wild man of outside broadcasts, monstrously talented but with the habit of making his BBC bosses dream of early retirement. When he wasn't actually working on a programme, he could rarely be found. He would disappear with a fishing rod into the wilds of Torridon for weeks on end, while departmental secretaries and assistant producers were given the job of trying to track him down. I remember one thoroughly brassed-off secretary who'd been on Begg-hunting duties for some days telling a full canteen in Kensington House that she thought she was supposed to be working for the world's premier broadcasting organisation, not as a frigging Indian scout.

There would be sightings – at a smart restaurant with Carol Thatcher, well down the brandy in the Officers' Mess in Perth, entertaining the press secretary from Buckingham Palace. Then the trail would go cold again. But like Superman he was always there when he was needed. At the last minute the BBC decided to carry live coverage of the ships leaving for the Falklands War. I was to be the commentator. The day before the ships sailed, Begg was still absent without leave. But just as the OB department was about to give somebody else the job, he sauntered along the quayside looking more dishevelled than normal and with a toothbrush ostentatiously decorating his top pocket. Three hours later he had the job sorted, the cameras placed, vast quantities of extra equipment ordered, the budget overspent and the snotty little Royal Navy PR man who'd been giving us all grief on a charge.

Budgets and Begg did not sit happily together. Even in the days when the majority of BBC producers were profligate, Begg was legendary. He persuaded channel controllers to commission extraordinary programmes with budgets many small countries would have been delighted to have. But that was still no reason not to overspend if production values demanded it.

So it was that we headed for Orkney to produce a live climbing programme. The veteran climber Joe Brown was to lead his daughter Zoe on an ascent of a crumbling skyscraper of rock – The Old Man of Hoy. The logistics kept Mike happy (and away from Torridon and Thatcherism) for months. The outside broadcast scanners and satellite ground station trucks filled a ferry from Scrabster. Tons of broadcasting equipment had to be transhipped onto the Island of Hoy, and then flown by helicopter to the cliff top and then across the void onto the stack itself. An army of riggers and engineers, cameramen and sound recordists had to be ferried in small boats between Kirkwall and Hoy. That was less of a problem that getting them safely back again once they'd been let loose on the ferryman's Viking Special – a sickly black home-brew mixture with half the recommended water and twice the sugar that could scramble the legs of the wildest rigger/driver. By the time they'd regained the power of speech and finished their rigging, the site around the commentary box looked like GCHQ as designed by Heath Robinson, with a huge lattice of aerials to allow us to hear what the climbers were saying. The first time Zoe lost her footing on the climb, we wished we couldn't hear them quite so well.

The night before the broadcast we had a bit of a shindig. Begg was working on the principle that, even if the programme fell to bits, at least we would have had the party. When I came down early the following morning, I found Joe Brown and Mo Antoine, who was going to be operating one of the cameras on the face of the Old Man, fast asleep on the pool table. They went directly from the green baize to the crumbling sandstone as if it was the most natural preparation for a challenge they could imagine.

The climbers made it to the top, the weather was kind, and the various live broadcasts through the day were really rather good. Glowing reviews took the edge off the overspend. Occupants of the sixth floor preened, having been told it was one of those programmes that only the brave BBC would dare to tackle.

Meanwhile, we were amusing the staff of British Airways Highland Division at Kirkwall Airport. Even in hard-drinking Orkney it's presumably unusual for forty broadcasters and broadcasting engineers to turn up for check-in straight from the party and each clutching a bottle of champagne. We filled about half the plane. The other half was occupied by heavily pregnant Orcadian ladies off for their antenatals in Aberdeen. The captain had enjoyed the programme the day before and offered to give us a treat, a view we wouldn't have seen of the Old Man of Hoy. We bounced round the island at what felt like about a hundred feet above an angry sea. As we approached the stack, everybody on the right of the plane got out of their seats and tried to get a better view through the left-hand windows. The plane lurched alarmingly. It was a spectacular sight, but I've often wondered how many young residents of Kirkwall put their premature delivery down to the day a BBC engineer ended up sitting on their mum's knee.

To cap the Old Man of Hoy, the following year we went to Ben Nevis to broadcast live coverage of a winter ice climb. In short order the preening stopped. From our attractive base camp on the municipal rubbish dump in Fort William we looked into a whiteout. The marines manning the camp on the summit were getting some of the best arctic training they'd had in years. Dave Clem, the helicopter pilot, whose proud boast was that he'd had forty-three engine outs and lived to tell the tale, shuttled in and out of the blizzard with nets of equipment slung beneath the Jet Ranger. Ten yards from the ground he disappeared. Only the thrum of the rotors competing with a dervish wind told us that he was still safely airborne.

We got most of the equipment onto the mountain and for three days sat tight to wait for a window in the weather. On Saturday morning it lifted, and in glorious sunshine I did a seven-minute programme trail into the Noel Edmonds Show. Shortly after Noel went home to Crinkly Bottom, the blizzards came back, and we got nothing more on the air. It must have been the most expensive programme trail in broadcasting history.

Begg drank as only a man with a family connection to a distillery possibly could. He was the perfect host at the wake after we abandoned Ben Nevis. Such a good night was had by all that next morning I had to think very hard to remember if the broadcast had gone out or not.

A refreshing lack of political correctness was another of Mike's great strengths. Not for him the whingeings of the human resources directorate. He was brutally blunt, often carpeted for offending incompetents, and one of the best bosses I've ever had the pleasure to work for (even though at times I fell below his expectations and into the incompetence department). He had a long-running spat with two of his fellow producers in the OB department. I'll spare their blushes in the wider world by only using their departmental nickname – the Tellytubbies. They were blah blah blah sort of chaps, pompous, charmless and evidently out of the country when the talent was distributed. I often had to work for them on state OBs such as Remembrance Sunday, when they'd posture their way through the broadcast apparently unaware that the vision mixer was doing their job for them while they indulged their cheerless hobby of being as offensive as possible to all and sundry.

When Begg produced one of those big occasions at the Cenotaph or Trooping the Colour or the fiftieth anniversary of Arnhem, he really produced. He understood and cared about the core values that the events embraced. Because of that, he made the commentator's job so much easier. There was a coherence to the broadcast which made it a story that lived again in the telling. The year I commentated at the Cenotaph with Begg in the producer's seat was the best outside broadcast performance I ever gave.

Sadly Michael Begg, like so many other talented people in the BBC, arrived at the sad but inevitable conclusion that he could no longer stomach the lunatic gobbledegook of the Birtian revolution. His job was being swamped in a mire of consultants, focus groups, politically correct and grammatically inadequate discussion papers, bosses who cravenly agreed with bad management decisions to protect their pensions, and, above all, a fundamental misunderstanding of what public service broadcasting was about. He retired early from the staff of Birt's New Model Army and took himself off to a lonely corner of East Anglia with a collie dog and a new wife.

Michael Begg was a royalist but not a sycophant. If some bit of royal ceremonial went pear-shaped, he would fire off a memo that could make Lord Chamberlains blanch. (Or should it be Lords Chamberlain? I really ought to know after all these years of practice.) It was said that officers of the parade feared Begg only slightly less than they feared the Queen and the Garrison Sergeant Major. On many occasions Begg's wrath was reserved for Major Sir Michael Parker, by appointment organiser of flummeries to Buckingham Palace and the Sultan of Brunei. The Galloping Major (TA) regularly produced the Royal Tournament. In its later years it got to look decidedly threadbare, in no small measure due to the swingeing reductions in the strength of the armed forces. I remember one year the two Michaels having a blazing row that was inadvertently broadcast over the Earls Court public address system. It was not conducted in language that would have passed muster in Clarence House, and I seem to remember that Begg's parting shot was along the lines of: 'If it gets any bloody smaller we're going to end up with the fucking Azerbaijani Marines as the star turn and there are only two of them.'

Speaking of Clarence House, Begg and I shared a fondness for the strange ways of the Queen Mother and her rather odd household. Trying to get information from Clarence House about an event in which Queen Elizabeth would feature was a bit like ringing up a rather chaotic old folks' home. The Queen Mother was nothing if not loyal, and you always got the impression that age and infirmity were no barrier to employment in her household.

Her Majesty was taking the salute one year at Beat Retreat on Horse Guards that Begg and I were covering. She left Clarence House late, and even a bit of a canter down the Mall couldn't make up sufficient time before she arrived at Horse Guards. Our live broadcast was already having to fill while we waited for the main event to start. The Queen Mother went to meet her guests in the Major General's office overlooking the parade ground, where they would watch the proceedings in comfort on television screens provided by the BBC. We waited and padded. I told tales of her fondness for the Scottish Castle of Mey (I seem to remember it was a Scottish regiment that was on parade). I told stories about her enduring appeal to the public, her love of embroidery, her fascination with horse breeding, her knowledge of Aberdeen Angus cattle and North Country Cheviot sheep, and anything else from memory, research or desperation that would fill the gap. Twenty minutes later she appeared, the band struck up, and the production assistant started negotiating with the Presentation department for an overrun.

A few days later, a message was relayed from Clarence House. Her Majesty apologised for the delay she'd caused. But she'd been enjoying my commentary so much that she just couldn't tear herself away from the television set.

CHAPTER TWELVE
THE DROVE

think the Queen Mother would have got on with Tom Purdham rather well. She could have talked to him about the merits of Cheviot sheep and black cattle. Pushing his cap back and leaning on his crook, he would have said 'Aye, maybe, Ma'am' in a tone that left his disapproval in no doubt, before suggesting that Herdwicks and Blue Grey cows were an altogether better bet.

It was a gamble letting Tom loose on Channel 4, but I needn't have worried. In about twenty minutes he'd managed to convince a Channel 4 commissioning editor that it was the most natural thing in the world to make a documentary recreating an eighteenth-century cattle drove from Scotland to London. I'd been working on the project for months and getting nowhere. In desperation I suggested that the make-or-break meeting should be at Tom's farm in Wasdale. The reasoning was that anyone who met Tom couldn't help but be hooked by his combination of Cumbrian fell farming bluntness and infectious enthusiasm (not to mention that it was an opportunity for the editor and his lady companion to break free of the stifling constraints of Charlotte Street and have a hooky weekend in the Lake District).

As we leaned over the gate of Tom's scruffy cattle pens in the Bengarth farmyard, the editor, whose name conveniently escapes me, said that he'd enjoyed his visit so much we could have £84,000 to make the programme. Tom's mouth dropped open, but he responded well to the kick on the shin. As he faked a coughing fit, I suggested, unconvincingly, that it was unlikely we could make the programme for such a pittance, but of course we'd try. The editor and his companion drove off into the sunset to find the nearest hotel, and Tom and I tried our best to rationalise the budget by having a whale of a night in the back bar of the Strands.

For years I knew Tom as Father Tom – ever since he adopted me at my own father's funeral. It was because of Tom that I ended up living in the Lake District (for which much thanks) and that I took up part-time farming (if I ever stop losing money, I may thank his memory for that, too). He was what they used to call 'a character', but that doesn't do anything like justice to his capacity to deliver up fun and fancy wherever he went.

I remember one afternoon heading off in Tom's barely legal British Leyland van to collect a ram for our newly acquired flock from a farm somewhere near Broughton-in-Furness. Tom warned me on the way that the farmer we were buying it from used to have a drink problem. We did the deal, and I was surprised he insisted we have a snifter to seal it. A bottle of Teachers had pride of place on the kitchen table. The farmer proceeded to pour whisky for Tom and me like only a reformed alcoholic could, vicariously savouring every drop we drank. When the bottle was finished we reeled off homeward, but by this stage Tom was fancying a night out. We went in search of Tucker Brown, a rotund and cheery neighbourhood sheep dealer. The resulting session carried on for some hours. We came out into a freezing early morning to find that the ram's breath had deposited half an inch of ice on the inside of the van's windows. The clattering van heater did its best but failed. It was not a comfortable night's sleep with Tom snoring on my shoulder and the ram dribbling down my neck. When I set off at first light Tom was instantly awake, running a thirst, and suggesting what he thought were suitably entertaining diversions on the way home. At seven in the morning, we were knocking up the landlord of the King's Head in Broughton and ordering coffee, whisky and a scoopful of rough mix for the ram. All three were provided without quibble. I should have realised that morning that *The Drove* was going to be a challenge for reasons other than coming in on budget.

We first had to buy our cattle. Tom, in his new role as Channel 4's livestock agent, was despatched to auction marts across the north of England and southern Scotland to find small black cattle that would bear some resemblance to the type of beasts the drovers would have shifted. Obviously not much has changed since the eighteenth century in places like Castle Douglas, because we had a herd gathered together at Bengarth in next to no time – mainly Galloways but with a handful of Highland cattle for no better reason than they looked prettier.

When the six Highlanders arrived in the Lake District, they came off the wagon like the Red Arrows. Within a quarter of an hour they were three fields away. I suggested to Tom that we may have a bit of a problem here. Dismissively, he assured me that within the month he'd have his droving herd so well trained that he'd be able to stop them at a red traffic light. (As it happened, during the filming he did just that at a busy road junction somewhere on the A5.) I felt slightly vindicated, though, because two of the Highlanders were so bloody minded they had to be left at home. In fact, it took Tom's son and me three weeks to catch them when eventually the time came to sell them on.

We set off from a farm near Newton Stewart, on one of the wettest day's filming I've ever experienced. It was the start of a journey that would take us across southern Scotland, over the hills to Malham in Yorkshire, then down the route of the A1 – the Great North Road. East to St Faith's near Norwich, which was the location of one of the biggest eighteenth-century cattle fairs, a site now occupied by Norwich Airport. East Anglian livestock fatteners would buy the cattle, which were thin after their long trek, feed them up on the new miracle ration – turnips – and then send them south along the route we'd take to London and Smithfield Market. A mere 380 miles.

On day one we did six. Ten was apparently the average stroll for the drovers, but they presumably bypassed the Bladnoch Distillery. Tom had spotted on the map that it was on our route, and passing a distillery without stopping was self-evidently a sin. Bladnoch is the only lowland malt, but (more important than that) until Tom's dying day we used to classify hangovers in units of Bladnochs, so comprehensive was that night's celebration of having actually started our adventure.

The director of *The Drove* was a rare chap indeed. Bill Cartner is a broadcaster and a gentleman. Over the years we must have made hundreds of programmes together, and I never once heard him say a bad word about anybody, however incompetent, unpleasant or annoying that body might be. I once accused him of saintly tendencies, but he said he was merely living proof of the emollient characteristics of Whisky Mac. But *The Drove* tested him. It was a logistical nightmare. Cows are marginally less trouble than television presenters, but it's rare to have to work with thirty-six presenters. Bill was having to spend as much time organising grazing permissions and cattle rations as he was directing the filming, but with never a complaint.

No, there was one. Cliff, the sound recordist, was worried about being able to pick up the signal from four or five radio mikes simultaneously, so in his garage at home he constructed an aerial of such proportions that we had to hire someone to carry it. Bill took one look at the monster lattice of aluminium tubes and wires and said that he didn't realise making contact with ET was part of the programme brief. In Bill's terms that was a complaint.

We didn't walk the cattle all the way. Our consultant vet said that modern beasts were nowhere near as tough as their eighteenth-century ancestors. And, anyway, in those days they used to shoe them. It seems they were better off than many eighteenth-century children. We rang Edward Martin, a master farrier at Closeburn, who said he'd never tried to shoe cattle but would have a go. He struggled. We put shoes on one Galloway for the sake of the filming, but for the sake of Edward Martin's sanity we left the rest alone. Bits of the journey would have to be done by cattle wagon. Bill found transport manager added to his portfolio of jobs.

At Longtown we had to ford the River Esk. Originally we were going to walk the cattle across the sands of the Solway Firth at low tide, until we went to meet the local haaf net fishermen to check out the route and discovered that the running tide came in at about thirty miles an hour. Our bravado ebbed.

The crossing of the Esk was dodgy enough. The cattle seemed to be quite enjoying it after several miles of dusty road work and frolicked about in the river. But neither Tom nor I could swim, and we certainly didn't frolic. Once the fast-running current was over our knees, the best we could do was hang onto each other in the fervent hope of not being swept away. Professional drovers we weren't, and the image was further dented when Tom stumbled ashore, fell to his knees and kissed the ground rather as the old Pope after braving Alitalia.

But it was a joyous trip, and I can still conjure up vignettes in which everyone is laughing. There was the morning when we lost every single cow in the mists of Malham Moor. Then the night in Norfolk when a couple of the young farmers who'd come to help with the droving got rather the worse for wear, ignored the old advice that the only two things in life one shouldn't attempt are incest and morris dancing, and tried to cavort with the St Faith's Morris Men. (Presumably what they were up to was incest because it certainly wasn't dancing). There was the cold night huddled round the campfire when our travelling companion, Ian Husband, had to sample the traditional droving fare of fried blood, onions and bean stew. 'I don't give a bugger what it's been. I'm just worried about what it is now, and more to the point what effect it's going to have on me tomorrow morning.'

Recently, Scotty – Eric Scott-Parker, the cameraman – reminded me of the evening in Daventry when we were celebrating some minor triumph on the project and got to bed very late after a hard night's planning. Scotty had been merrily charging his drinks all night to room 17, and knew he'd had a bit too much when he went upstairs and couldn't even find his toothbrush. It wasn't until the next morning that he realised he should have been in room 17 in a different hotel. And there was the occasion when it was suggested to Tom that the drovers' method of keeping warm on wintry nights – throwing their plaid into an icy steam and then wrapping themselves in it – would make a good sequence for the film. He slowly rearranged his flat cap, walked across to the cattle, and had an intense conversation with a bemused Galloway on the subject of directors who'd gone native.

Perhaps we threw ourselves into the project with such gusto because we were aware of a shadow that moved in the background of so many of the scenes. Brian Anderson, a real friend and the man who researched most of the programme, had been involved in the freakest of freak accidents while working out our route beside the A1. He was walking across a field thirty yards from the road when an articulated lorry went out of control, crossed the central reservation, mounted the embankment and mowed him down. Brian was killed instantly. *The Drove* had to be good for Brian's sake.

A month's filming later, we arrived in London. The City of London Police insisted we do the last lap to Smithfield very early one Sunday morning to cause as little disruption to traffic as possible. Another condition was that we paid for a Corporation dust cart to follow along behind and clear up any 'little mistakes', as someone in the press office put it so inanely.

Tom was incensed. He stomped about in his clogs, kicking debris along the gutters. He thundered that he certainly wasn't going to let his cattle wander about belly deep in Coca-Cola tins, McDonald's wrappers and probably hypodermics if he was to look closely enough. It was a bit of an overreaction but we got his drift. The cattle meanwhile just stood about weighing up the buildings that towered around them, occasionally sniffing at the remains of some distant relative in a burger wrapper, and chewing the cud of their unusually early Hertfordshire breakfast.

Tom was mollified, and we set off to plod through Little Britain behind Barts Hospital and past the house where John Betjeman used to live. It's a shame we were a few years too late to give him a spot of early morning inspiration. But just round the corner from Betjeman's house, the whole drove came to a sudden stop as a black BMW wheeled round the corner. It shuddered to a halt in front of us just a few feet away from the four spectacular sets of horns of the Highlanders that had appointed themselves herd leaders. The couple in the car were in evening dress and presumably on their way home from a party. After a longish pause, the driver shook his head and reversed slowly away, obviously making a mental note never again to drink whatever he'd been drinking last night.

The smell of blood from the meat market must have drifted on the breeze, so Tom said, because the cattle were getting edgy.

For the first time in almost 380 miles they were difficult to control, holding back and trying to turn away in the narrow streets. Tom shushed and whispered to them, running his hand along sleek backs, and they settled well enough to let us gather them under the wrought iron vaults of Smithfield at journey's end. We posed for team photographs, celebrated on machine coffee bought from a stall across the road (having managed to comprehensively overspend the budget), and then headed home.

There was a postscript. My final, unlikely production task was to organise the auction of the cattle (which, if it went well, might just sort out our overspend). Despite farming's rough and ready image, a charming, old-fashioned gentility survives in the world of cattle auctioneering. Messrs Harrison & Hetherington of Carlisle announced in the local press something to the effect that:

> We are honoured with the sale of thirty-six prime Galloway, Blue Grey and Highland bullocks and heifers as seen in the documentary *The Drove* on behalf of Channel 4 television.

The auctioneers coped with the whole business entirely professionally, which is more than can be said for Channel 4's accountants, who couldn't get their heads round the fact that £14,500 of their money was still on the hoof.

There was a big turnout of buyers, who came not so much to see the stars of the show but because they assumed Channel 4 would be a soft touch. We weren't and we got a good price. Even the two renegade Highlanders that we hadn't managed to calm sufficiently to take on the trip with us sold well. They were bought by a chap who planned to turn them out onto the unfenced Burgh Marsh on the Solway coast. To this day he's probably still trying to round them up.

CHAPTER THIRTEEN
GOD'S COUNTRIES

It was during the making of *The Drove* that I found Crag House. To be more accurate, Tom found Crag House. Annette and I had been trying to buy a small farm in the Lake District for some months, but had always come second at the various auctions. In desperation, we'd gone to look at a smallholding with the ominous name of Boad Hole. Its name didn't do justice to the horrors we found there. It was a windswept, leaking cottage in the middle of fifteen acres of Lakeland swamp. Alfred Hitchcock would have salivated about it as a film location. I joked about the potential of digging trout lakes and breeding water buffalo. Annette muttered under her breath that even a suggestion of purchase would result in divorce. As we weren't yet married, I took it as a serious threat. We told the farmer who was selling it that it looked just the sort of place we'd dreamed of and ran away before Anthony Perkins appeared out of the attic.

One damp weekend shortly after our escape from Boad Hole, Tom took us to see an empty National Trust farmhouse with two huge and semi-derelict ranges of stone buildings, holes in the roof, a river in the farmyard, no land to speak of, and rats in the gloaming. It was obviously perfect because Annette didn't threaten divorce. The approach to it was by a long and rather dreary track, but its backdrop was of Buckbarrow and Kirk Fell, Great Gable and Scafell Pike, and the Wastwater Screes. All these years later and having seen that view thousands of times, we still reckon we've got the best backyard in Britain.

It took almost two years to get the place habitable with the help of Jim The Animal. Jim was a Stockport navvy, on the run at the time from the Department of Social Security. Despite his nickname and trailing knuckles demeanour, he was one of the softest men I've ever met. Except when he wielded a pick or was put in charge of negotiating a deal. He took me on excursions into secret quarters of Manchester that appeared on no map, and where clans of McGintys and Macnamaras (their names have been changed to protect the guilty) seemed to run a thriving parallel economy independent of such minor encumbrances as the Revenue and the Customs and Excise. Here, long after the entirely unreasonable introduction of decimalisation, we would pay fourpence threefarthings a foot for roofing timber from demolished schools, and two and ninepence a block for building stone from redundant old folks' homes. I couldn't shake off the image of kiddies turning up on a Monday morning and old folk coming back from the Evergreen Club to find their buildings gone, spirited away to the Lake District on a dodgy wagon (again supplied by one of Jim's shadowy Celtic associates).

It was in Jim's company that I discovered a gentle therapy that really ought to be offered on the NHS to all those unfortunates who apparently need counselling nowadays. Just sit them on a barn loft on a wet winter's afternoon and get them to de-nail a few thousand feet of reclaimed timber.

The de-nailing therapy was particularly useful to me at the time, because the reconstruction of Crag House was interspersed with work on a new broadcasting venture – a series for the Religious Affairs department in London. A more unchristian bunch of broadcasters it would have been hard to find. The programme, *Sunday Night*, was one of those undercover religious shows pretending to be current affairs in the hope of hanging onto that bit of the audience that hits the off button at the first whiff of surplice.

It got off to a bad start. Rehearsals were dominated by an increasingly acrimonious debate about Venetian blinds, which are obviously a theological hot topic. The blinds dominated the set. Behind them was an array of expensive photo blow-ups of the London evening skyline. But should the blinds be open, closed or ajar? At production meetings every position had its supporters. Unfortunately, nowhere near as much effort was being devoted to the minor matter of editorial content.

Week after week we fell onto the air with features of such superficiality that *Supermarket Sweep* would have rejected them. By week six, when I lodged a small protest about an item which was the religious equivalent of the skateboarding duck (you'll have to be old enough to remember a programme called *Nationwide* to make sense of that reference), the atmosphere was so bad that St Michael and all his angels would have been hard pressed to reunite the warring factions. The minute the programme was finished I did a runner, avoiding the Lime Grove hostility suite. I chose instead the more appealing option of sitting among the pigeons on Euston Station for three hours until it was time for the sleeper service to Carlisle.

That's how I met Mr Gopal and the Nepalese royal family. One Sunday evening, peckish after a hard weekend's religious warfare, I wandered out from Euston into Eversholt Street to find a restaurant. At first sight it didn't look promising. But between a down-at-heel gent's hairdressers and the British Transvestite Centre was The Great Nepalese. What it lacked in the way of neighbours, it made up for with its impeccable hospitality. Mr Gopal advanced with outstretched hand saying that here, surely, was a man who needed a drink; here was a man he must feed and cherish. Over the years I've got to know Mr

ABOVE: Grandfather 'Simmon' seated on a bench at Newcastleton Station.

RIGHT: The poor women of Canterbury (*Murder in the Cathedral*): Eric Robson top left; Roger Bolton top right; Roger Liddle bottom left.

Nessie with Eric aged four.

Jimmy in the Scots Guards.

LEFT: Father Tom.

BELOW: *The Drove*: the wettest day's filming.

RIGHT: The end of *The Drove* at Smithfield Market: Eric Robson, Tom Purdham, Ian Husband and Rob.

RIGHT BELOW: The Crag House ruins before renovation.

LEFT ABOVE: With AW during the filming of the BBC series.

LEFT: With film crew in Delhi to interview His Holiness the 14th Dalai Lama.

ABOVE: *Gardener's Question Time*: Anne Swithinbank, Pippa Greenwood, Geoffrey Smith, Eric Robson, Bob Flowerdew.

LEFT: Geoffrey Smith, Eric Robson, Betty Boothroyd and Pippa Greenwood. Being shown round the Speaker's house after a recording of GQT having just been objectionable about Madam Speaker's poinsettias.

BELOW: Recording with Bunny Guiness at the *GQT* garden in Hampshire.

TOP: Filming for the Fiftieth Anniversary of Arnhem.

ABOVE: The Century Theatre, Carlisle.

Gopal well. I've heard regular news of his family in Wimbledon and Kathmandu and his battles with the planners of Camden Town.

But one evening he was on edge when I arrived. He took me to one side and, like a supporting actor in a Bollywood musical, whispered, 'Tonight my prince has come', indicating a group of heavies making a fair old racket in the furthest corner. I was ushered to the table. A chap who turned out to be the playwright Willy Russell (another sleeping car refugee in Eversholt Street) stood up to let me into the spare seat, and I found myself sitting between him and the Crown Prince of Nepal. It didn't take long to realise why Willy Russell had left a gap. With profoundest apologies to Mr Gopal, his prince was a loud-mouthed slob, a spoilt brat in Armani suit and Roy Orbison shades.

Some years later, when news shuddered round the world that in a fit of alcoholic madness he'd shot most of the rest of his family in the royal palace in Kathmandu, I confess I wasn't surprised. It's a pity, though, that we weren't still doing *Sunday Night*, because the massacre would have made a canny item on the programme and allowed us to explore the inconsistencies of reincarnation in Nepalese Buddhism. Which, of course, is a remark in extremely bad taste, unlike Mr Gopal's Haku Choyala followed by chicken with green chillies.

You've probably gathered I could have been more selective about the programmes I've agreed to work on over the years. But when only a few producers are beating a path to the outside broadcaster's door, and the path in question happens to be full of very large and expensive holes waiting for drains, plumbing and electrical wiring to be inserted, even the naffest ideas take on a certain mercenary charm. Which I suppose is why I ended up as the commentator at the opening of the Humber Bridge (a job which involved weeks of research, mainly mugging up on rivets), why I happily thought of suitable banalities to accompany performances of the dancing diggers at the Royal Highland Show in Edinburgh for a couple of years (although I eventually had a 'no dancing diggers' clause inserted in my contract), and why I agreed to co-present an embarrassing BBC 2 New Year's Eve extravaganza with Keith Chegwin in Manchester. This was long before Mr Chegwin decamped first to a drying out clinic and then to a satellite station to present a quiz show in the nude, but even with his clothes on he wasn't an edifying spectacle. Prancing about on an open air stage in sub-zero temperatures introducing perished acts to an audience getting their stimulation from the bottle rather than the show, neither was I.

Then a spot of luck. I was given the chance to join the reporting team on a programme called *File On 4*, which was (and still is) a beacon in the pervading broadcasting gloom. It was a tough programme to work on, and Colin Adams was a tough editor to work for. Producing forty minutes of polished, single-subject radio a week was challenging. The world was its patch, and it set the agenda rather than merely following it. And all produced by a handful of raffish reporters, three producers, an editor and the Miss Moneypenny of the production office, Lindsay Alker.

Lindsay was the power behind the microphone whose favourite put-down was 'Bloody *Editors*, who needs them?' For *Editors* substitute *Reporters*, *Producers*, *Directors General* or *Men*, depending on the circumstances. I eventually discovered that Lindsay's growl was worse than her nibble, but when I first joined the programme she scared the shit out of me.

When I say *File On 4* toured the world, that treat (as I thought of it at the time) was generally reserved for the old hands. As the novice, I would be despatched from Lindsay's office to places like Ashington and Wrexham. I still vividly remember spending a fortnight in Wrexham one weekend. In the evenings the producer and I would huddle in some grim pub or other while the locals pointedly conversed in Welsh. On the second night I cracked. I loudly berated the good citizens of Wales for having raised ignorance to an art form and confusing sheep with leisure centres. The lady producer shushed and blushed, but I said loudly that it obviously didn't matter because they couldn't speak our bloody language anyway. They still didn't speak to us, but at least it encouraged them to talk to each other in English.

At the end of a week's recording, producer and reporter would come back with hours of tape that had to be assembled in short order into a story comprehensible even to the casual listener. In forty minutes we would attempt to unravel the economic ills of the health service or explain the complexities of the flags of convenience system behind which lurked the brutalities of the international maritime trade. We'd run our best efforts past Colin Adams, who instantly spotted the flaws and inconsistencies and set about correcting them, generally when we were just about to go on air. Colin loved the buzz of the deadline. We would regularly be in the position of part one of the programme going out while Colin was in another edit channel nipping and tucking part two, and looking forward to getting the couple of minutes' overrun out of part three. Meanwhile, I'd be in the Manchester studio doing the links live.

I got to be quite good at the job, but others – like Gerry Northam and Michael Robinson – were better. I used to listen to their programmes and envy their gentle delivery, their simple but subtle turn of phrase, and their softly spoken questions that made the villain or the evasive politician squirm. Gerry, who dressed rather in the manner of a rural dean, also worked as a producer for a while. It was with him that I made a programme, first for radio and eventually for television, that I can still replay on demand and still find chilling in its tale of institutional brutality. Gerry had negotiated for us to be allowed into the Moss Side and Ashworth Special Hospitals at Maghull on the outskirts of Liverpool. Like Rampton and its Scottish equivalent at Carstairs, they were hospitals in name only. Its nurses were warders, members of the Prison Officers' Association. Its inmates were classed as criminally insane.

The programme could so easily have been *Zoo Quest* with us looking through the bars at the caged exhibits. But what we found was a sink of despair and lost lives that we tried to portray as openly and honestly as possible. Certainly, there was an undercurrent of evil. The Moors murderer Ian Brady was confined in Moss Side, as was Graham Rose, who had cheerily poisoned his workmates. But the majority of the patients we talked to were at worst inadequate and, despite the numbing influence of the chemical cosh Largactyl, remarkably normal. They certainly seemed more normal than many of the psychiatric staff. One psychiatrist we met at Moss Side had a disconcerting habit of talking to herself and spitting at patients in the corridors.

In Ashworth there were wards full of old ladies who'd been locked up for perhaps sixty years because they'd been pregnant and unmarried and their fathers took that to be an obvious sign of madness. The state happily offered its services to underpin those fine Edwardian family values. In Moss Side we met Harold, who sat on a windowsill and sang a plaintiff nursery song for us. He'd been locked away at the age of six because he'd stolen sixpence from his dad's mantelpiece and was therefore classed as a moral defective. While we were there, he clocked up seventy years of confinement. With most of them the institution had done its job so well that they would have been incapable of living outside after all those years. The ward was virtually all they knew and probably all they could cope with.

But what was most scary about the Special Hospital was the

experimentation. It was a playpen for psychologists. A place where all manner of theories could be tested to destruction on a captive audience. We were invited to see one experiment which claimed to be making a breakthrough in the understanding of sex offending. The theory advanced by the psychologists (and which they were setting out to prove) was that some sex offenders have a full-blown erection – perhaps an unfortunate phrase – before they realise they're having one and that leads them into trouble. To test the theory, a number of inmates were wired up each Tuesday afternoon to rubber penile rings and then shown dirty videos of everything from bestiality to violent interracial sex supplied from stocks conveniently held by the local video library, otherwise known as the police station. The idea was that the penile rings would register whenever an erection occurred, and the inmate would press a button when he thought he had one. The scientists (for so they considered themselves to be) were sure the button would be pressed after the ring moved. It invariably was – and for two very good reasons that the inmates were happy to explain to us. First of all, they would always masturbate at Tuesday lunchtime and, second, they very soon realised that the moment they pressed the button the video stopped. An afternoon of officially sanctioned dirty movies being preferable to an afternoon on the ward, the button could wait.

After a week on the wards and despite our best attempts to be professional and objective, I think everyone on the crew began to think of the Special Hospital rather as you might think of Battersea Dog's Home. We'd all met a patient we wanted to give a good home to. Sad and gentle old men whose only threat to the order of things was that they put their underpants on back to front, forgetful old ladies with nervous smiles who could have been your granny. After a fortnight we were evangelical in our demands that a rotten system had to be changed.

The programmes told a powerful story and achieved precisely nothing. There was a report some years later that condemned the regime in Moss Side and Ashworth, but, as I remember, it was mainly on the grounds that the nurses, members of the Prison Officers' Association, had too much power and that they weren't giving value for money. So far as I'm aware, nobody rescued Harold.

One of the little burdens of appearing on television and radio is that people often accuse you of having too much power. The accusation normally surfaces after the third pint or the second bottle of red wine.

'Power without responsibility' rumbles up from the other end of the dinner table, and there follows the predictable litany of complaints.

'It's trial by television I object to.'

'Jeremy Paxman thinks he's more important than the Prime Minister.'

'Somebody should tell John Humphrys he's not elected.'

'Of course, it's obvious that children are being damaged by the television programmes they watch.'

'The programmes you let them watch, surely?'

Oh, dear, you've risen to the bait, and however diverse the assembled company, invariably you find yourself in a minority of one. Maybe that's why so many national broadcasters live in the laagers of Clerkenwell and Islington, and have their holiday cottages cheek by jowl in West Cork and Tuscany. Safety in dinner party numbers.

So, ignoring tales of the corrosive effect of Big Brother and accusations that Thought for the Day is a left-wing papist plot (and there's a concept to grapple with), allow me a moment to say that the media have nowhere near as much power as most of their viewers and listeners seem to think. Television may be able to sell washing powder, but it doesn't bring down governments. Jim Callaghan and John Major are the boys for that.

In all the programmes I've made over the years, I can think of only two that directly changed public policy. One scotched the building of a particularly nasty and inappropriately named fine chemicals plant in West Cumbria when I reported that the only other complex of its sort in Europe was not only dangerous but losing money hand over fist. Subsequently, the site was turned into a wind farm, and no doubt the good people of Siddick on the Cumberland coast remember me in their prayers for that.

The other was a programme that argued the case for a modern canal system. A network of commercial waterways would allow freight to be carried on barges from the industrial heartlands of northern England (when there still were some) deep into Europe. The government had set its face against the plan. Our programme persuaded it to fund the development of the Sheffield and South Yorkshire Navigation. Sir Frank Price, Chairman of the British Waterways Board, was so delighted he invited me to the opening, where I was interviewed by a man who described himself as the opera and canals correspondent of Radio Sheffield. He was a jolly cove and we two outside broadcasters had a thoroughly pleasant afternoon.

But if the programmes I made for *File On 4* weren't going to change the world, at least one of them did give a timely warning of horrors to come. With the producer Stuart Simon, an erudite and buttoned up man of private means who I always suspected worked under sufferance with this ill-educated and working class reporter, I set off for the Middle East to report on the plight of the Palestinians against a background of increasing tension in Israel.

At the risk of further inflaming the prejudices of my anti-television friends, I have to be honest and say that reporting is a subjective business, albeit informed by fact and event. It's impossible not to be affected by the people you meet and the way they advance their argument as well as the merit of the argument itself. So it was in Jerusalem. The Israeli politicians and lobbyists we met were all thoroughly unpleasant. The more senior the more objectionable, until we arrived at the office of Foreign Minister Yitzhak Shamir, who was the most unpleasant of the lot. Squat and neckless, he sat behind his desk like an ogrous escapee from a Grimm's fairy tale. While the tape wasn't running, he dribbled poison. The Palestinians were interlopers, animals, scum. When the tape started, he was more measured but still threatened retribution against the organisers of Palestinian resistance. It was a moment of parallel reality. Here I was sitting across a desk from a man who'd been operations director of the Jewish Nationalist Stern Gang during the Second World War, who'd organised the killing of Lord Moyne, British Minister Resident for the Middle East in 1944. A man who that morning lectured me on the evils of armed resistance.

The following day we flew to Beirut via Cairo. The Jerusalem to Cairo service had been established as one of the practical benefits of the Camp David accords, the only direct air link between Israel and an Arab country. It was scarcely normal. A completely unpainted commercial jet gleamed aluminium silver on the tarmac, and aboard were just three other paying customers. The service was seen as a legitimate target by terrorists opposed to Egyptian President Sadat's attempts at a peace process. The safety demonstration about bracing positions and what to do in the event of crash landing on water seemed more relevant than on most flights. But we made it. We changed to a rather jollier Middle East Airlines service in Cairo and flew into the wreckage of Beirut.

Like tinnitus, I can still hear the eerie whistling of the St George Hotel towering above the harbour. The wind from the Mediterranean whining through shell-buckled metal window frames and flapping the shredded Venetian blinds. That evening in the Commodore Hotel, where we were staying and which had only lost its top floor to the artillerymen of the Maronite Christian forces during the Lebanese civil war, we joined the huddle of international journalists round the basement bar. Among them was Bob Fisk, a fine writer and sometimes unkindly described as a war zone junkie. As only a professional in command of his subject could be, he was generous with his advice and with his contacts. When that same evening the bag containing my passport, tickets and travellers' cheques was stolen from the bar, it was Bob who had a mate at the embassy who could whistle up a new passport. Bob also knew someone in the interior ministry who owed him a favour and would organise the accompanying exit visas. He also reckoned that because of my dark complexion and beard, my passport would be particularly valuable in the Arab terrorist market.

The visit to the embassy next day was a bit like stepping into a William Boyd novel. The building was ominously ringed with concrete blocks to prevent suicide bomb attacks. Inside was a sunny Home Counties drawing room where I took tea with the press attaché and chatted about cricket, Mrs Thatcher and fell walking in the Lake District. When we eventually got round to the boring detail about a new passport, he explained that the official wheels grind exceeding slow but, it being December, he'd do his very best to get me home for Christmas, dear boy.

Replacing the lost travellers' cheques was more problematic. Miss Moneypenny had wired Thomas Cook, but their office happened to be in Maronite East Beirut across the Green Line manned by rather trigger-happy Syrian troops. Ahmed, our driver, said the only way of getting there without having to wait weeks for official permission that might never come was to smuggle me across. I sweated on the floor in the back of his car under a carpet, Ahmed greased the appropriate palm at the security checkpoint, and on the way to Thomas Cook he cheerily told me he'd done the dodgy crossing so many times that he called his car the number 47 bus.

Ahmed was a jolly, rotund man who beamed with pride as he handed round photographs of his innumerable children. Shortly after our return from the Middle East, we heard he'd been killed when his car ran over a land mine. I suppose it was only a matter of time. Ahmed's patch was one of the most volatile places on earth. He took us to the refugee camps of Sabra and Shatila, nursing his ancient Cadillac through potholed streets protected by concrete-filled metal drums to the ramshackle breeze-block houses of the Palestinian diaspora. Later, the official blind eye to the slaughter in those camps would become one of the worst stains on Israel's tarnished reputation.

Everywhere we went distant explosions and gunfire echoed through the narrow, overhanging streets. We decided to visit a Palestinian military training camp in the Cité Sportif, the Lebanese national sports stadium, and the sound of artillery fire in the hills reverberated round the tiers of empty seats. The Lebanese seemed singularly unconcerned by the war next door. While we recorded, Ahmed lay down in the east stand with a handkerchief over his face and snored.

The Palestinians we met in the camps showed a similar resignation. The battle would surely come, and they had to take time out to train for it. The group we met at the stadium, learning the techniques of house-to-house fighting, was made up of day-release doctors and university lecturers, writers and accountants. They told me that the Palestinians were the best educated of all the Arab peoples, with a higher percentage of them going to university than in most European countries. Denied a Palestinian state, they carried one in their head. During a break I saw a man sitting quietly reading *Titus Groan* in English who, a moment before, had been hurling himself into hand-to-hand combat.

But how could these cultured family men happily share cause with the wild-eyed leaders of groups like the Popular Front for the Liberation of Palestine, who regarded Israeli women and children as legitimate soft targets, and who would murder until kingdom (or revolutionary republic) come? Their answer – that bad things happen in every struggle for self-determination – and their checklist of rehearsed examples – Northern Ireland, Vietnam, Dresden – were a disappointment.

That night Ahmed took us to what at first sight seemed to be a derelict cinema, but as we approached through the dark alleyways it murmured like a disturbed hive. He warned us not to speak. Inside, it was packed to the doors with a crowd being orchestrated from ecstasy to hatred by the PFLP's founder, George Habash. I whispered to Stuart, the producer, that I'd like to record my impressions of the gathering. A man on the end of the nearest row, who a moment before had been on his feet applauding wildly, leaned across. In an accent which wouldn't have been out of place in the bar of the Randolph Hotel in Oxford, he suggested that would be a singularly bad idea. Tiny acts of kindness so unlike the bluster of the Israelis a week earlier.

Later, in the hotel bar, Bob Fisk suggested we'd been chancing our arm, which was a bit rich coming from a man who'd once hitched a lift on a tank to get closer to a battle in the Bekaa Valley. But having decided we might be proper reporters after all, he invited us to dinner, which we of course would pay for because the BBC had more brass than the *Independent*. Ahmed was summoned, and we drove off into a dark and potholed quarter of the city where it seemed almost every house was pocked by mortar fire. We bumped over a heap of rubble into an even narrower street. On what was left of the pavement, a pool of light illuminated a single round table complete with chintz cloth and a small posy of flowers – a restaurateur's two fingers to civil wars and ethnic conflict. Inside the French restaurant we were treated to a majestic dinner served with the panache that once marked out Beirut as the Paris of the eastern Mediterranean. After several bottles of Château Musar, produced against impossible odds each year by Gaston Hochar from his family vineyards in the Bekaa Valley, we stumbled out into the night. The sporadic rattle of automatic weapons had failed to disturb Ahmed, who was curled up in the back seat of the Cadillac fast asleep.

When the programmes went out, they predicted that Israel would invade Lebanon, and reported that because the Palestinians had nowhere to go but into the sea, they would have to stand and fight. We said it would be a bloody encounter, but we failed to predict the scale of the horror of what in 1982 Israel disingenuously called Operation Peace for Galilee.

Ahmed didn't live to smell the hundreds of decomposing corpses in Sabra and Shatila. He was no longer sleeping in the stands when the Israelis and their Lebanese Phalangist partners herded still more hundreds of Palestinians into the Cité Sportif, from where they were taken away for interrogation by Shin Beth, the Israeli secret service. Many of those prisoners were never seen again.

A random image still comes back in bleak dreams. On the dusty floor of what must once have been a sports stadium but is now a broken-toothed ruin lies a torn and crumpled copy of *Titus Groan*.

Another. At Beirut International Airport the morning Stuart and I were heading home for Christmas, Ahmed shook my hand and warned me to watch out for muggers in London. He'd heard it was a dangerous city.

CHAPTER FOURTEEN
FARMING

Amazingly, both telephone calls came on the same day. One from Tyne Tees Television to ask if they'd got the right number and did I know anything about farming, because they were looking for a new presenter for their series *Farming Outlook*. The other from BBC Birmingham inviting Eric Robinson to come to see them about a new farming programme they were going to make called *Countryfile*. I hadn't the slightest idea quite why the outside broadcaster had suddenly become the agricultural flavour of the month.

The interviews turned out to be as baffling. At Tyne Tees they seemed singularly uninterested in farming but wanted me to do a screen test. For some reason, they couldn't make the studio work that morning. Not a good omen, I remember thinking at the time. They coughed and shuffled for a bit, and then decided to offer me the job without a screen test. We still hadn't talked about farming. I told them I'd let them know if I could fit agricultural broadcasting into an already busy schedule and headed for the Midlands.

In Birmingham the producer spent the afternoon asking me what sort of farming programme I'd like to make. Did I have any ideas? (He certainly didn't seem to have any himself.) And to round things off, could I just canter through the Common Agricultural Policy for him? Of all the questions, that was the daftest. You'd be hard pressed to find a Minister of Agriculture, let alone a jobbing broadcaster, who knows how the Common Agricultural Policy works. But they offered me the job anyway, and I set off to drive home not a jot the wiser about what sort of programme they wanted me to present.

For no better reason than not liking either Birmingham or the M6, I picked Tyne Tees. John Craven got *Countryfile* and the Land Rover Discovery. I got Bob Farnworth, which was a much better deal. Bob looked like a Blaydon Races bookie. He sported the sort of wildly checked jacket with bright red paisley handkerchief in the top pocket that flagged up 'country' if not quite 'county'. His shock of wavy hair became more and more unruly for six months at a stretch, and then disappeared as if he'd just done one in Strangeways. He spent days puffing on his pipe and working his expenses as the piles of administrative paperwork rose to a level where they could more efficiently slide from his desk. From time to time he'd just disappear. When he emerged from his retreat looking rather tired, he'd tell us he'd been working on an interesting and important item which never seemed to make it into the programme.

A new and enthusiastic presenter must have been a burden to him. At first, I thought he was bone idle. As the years went by, I realised he was a finely tuned creative machine geared to the demands of modern television production. Make it cheap, make it fast, and make what the advertisers want. He also had an uncanny instinct for what the viewers actually wanted to see, as opposed to what television executives imagined they wanted to see, and proved those four aims were surprisingly compatible. *Farming Outlook* gathered in a substantial audience, far bigger than the diminishing numbers of farmers would suggest it should. He made farming interesting to people who thought milk was manufactured by Tesco. Later, we tried the same trick with everything from politics to economics. Quite often we succeeded. When we eventually got round to doing gardening programmes, we hit the jackpot.

That was a programme called *Earthmovers*, which I always thought made it sound like one of those big boys' toys programmes on the Discovery Channel. It was an instant hit with northern gardeners. As with all Bob's programmes, it was disarmingly, idly simple. In each half of the programme we'd wander round somebody's garden – sometimes stately, sometimes semi-detached – and capture the enthusiasm of the person who'd made it. No fancy graphics, no pacey music, no gimmicks, no makeovers. It was a programme about plants and people. Any decade now, when gardening programme producers stop trying to outdo each other in their quest for the most fragrantly fatuous presenter and the graphics most likely to bring on epilepsy, it's a style that might be rediscovered.

But first there was agriculture. I loved working on the programme. It chimed with the other bit of my life at Crag House, where building renovation had at last given way to part-time farming. We kept a small herd of suckler cattle and bred Derbyshire Gritstone sheep, pedigree Tamworth pigs and Clydesdale horses. Annette did the bulk of the work, with occasional time off to give birth to Lauren, Nicholas and Victoria. She had a bit of help from occasional farm assistants. Erica, who lived in a caravan with a swarm of dogs and rarely washed. Dawn, who filled a set of jodhpurs better than anyone else I've ever met. And Mark, who married into a West Cumbrian evangelical sect led by a chap with a mid-Atlantic accent and a white suit. Mark was about as reliable as Jeffrey Archer and complained constantly. All in all, a fairly standard rural idyll cast list. But when Annette was feeding horses with one hand and mucking out pigs with the other while at the same time having a baby at the breast, the phrase 'rural idyll' apparently didn't spring immediately to mind.

The first Christmas at Crag House was the nadir of Annette's farming career. A couple of months earlier she had been the star of the show, one of the BBC's top unit managers. There was a grand party to mark her departure to rural Cumberland – her flight into the land of Laura Ashley. Then, in mid-December, she could be found standing in the drizzle beside the farm van parked outside New Broadcasting House, Manchester, waiting for people to come out and collect the free range turkeys they'd ordered from us. (Lest you think I was shirking, I was doing a similar job at Border TV in Carlisle and the BBC in Newcastle. In our early farming days the only customers we could think of were our one-time broadcasting colleagues.) When we arrived home from our respective deliveries, we were not humming 'Hark the Herald Angels Sing' and we gave up mass poultry production soon after.

I'd farm at weekends and learn about farming during the week as I tramped the north of England interviewing Belgian Blue breeders and pig geneticists, experts in the diseases of goats' feet, equine acupuncturists and poultry psychologists. That last one is wishful thinking. I never did find anyone who was counselling hens, but as there seems to be a counsellor for everything else these days it's probably only a matter of time. The equine acupuncturist (for he did exist) came closest. He showed me with some pride a seven-volume Chinese publication about acupuncture of the hen.

On Saturday nights in the pub I'd cheerily tell Father Tom about the latest developments in state-of-the-art farming. Mostly he'd tell me they were bloody stupid ideas that would never catch on.

'Goats' feet. *Genetic manipulation*. Bollocks. Stockholm tar's what you want.'

I wish I'd known that when I spent a boring half-day with the man for whom goats' feet were an evangelical mission.

'If you want to do a programme about real bloody farming,' Tom would say in his cups, 'I'll do one for you.' Tom was never one for hiding his light under a feed sack. One of the benefits of freelancing is that if you feel strongly about a particular programme idea, you can keep on pushing it until some commissioning editor or other cracks. I wanted to call Tom's bluff and make a programme about the real farming life of a Lakeland valley, as opposed to the picture postcard images that we all know. I tried to sell the idea to several television stations. No takers. But eventually I managed to persuade Radio 4 that it was the gritty, actuality sort of documentary they ought to be making. *The Shepherd's Tale* was the result, and it followed Tom for a year on the Lakeland fells. Lambing time to lambing time.

When I first met Tom he'd eased up on work. He had sons to do that sort of thing. But much earlier he'd had a life that would have broken lesser men. His first farm was at Hayring, a poor, bleak place on the fringe of Alston Moor that he worked with his new wife Edna, who was considerably more fertile than the farm. All those years later, Edna would sit in the farmhouse kitchen at Bengarth and tell tales of working their fingers to the bone. The time when she was eight months pregnant and let the horse and muck cart run away. Tom had been aboard griping muck onto the field and emerged displeased (for which read raging) and covered in cowshit from head to foot. The day with a baby on her back that she crawled a field for six hours thinning turnips. Through all these stories, she'd smile a white-haired smile and remember hard and romantic times. But Hayring didn't make a living, so Tom took a second job as a lead miner. Up long before first light to feed the stock, he'd drive the bus to collect a shift of miners before doing his own eight hours underground. Then, having delivered his mates home, he'd go back to work on the farm in the dark before falling into a welcoming bed. This he did six days a week. Tom always used to say that poverty had been good to him. It kept him from his worst excesses.

For *The Shepherd's Tale* we spent weeks together recording anecdote and incident. If the programme had been given a television budget, we might just have made a profit. On radio money it was a celebration of friendship.

Half a lifetime later, some of the recording days for *The Shepherd's Tale* are still etched in memory. An April morning when we found a day-old lamb with its tongue and eyes taken by crows but still excruciatingly alive. Tom picked it up by its back legs and broke its head on a stone. A dead newborn lamb deftly skinned and the skin stretched over an orphan lamb to encourage a mother with milk to accept it as her own. The afternoon we spotted a ewe obviously ill and staring at death in a hedge bottom. Tom the hard man said it was about time I learned to sort a simple problem like a sheep with a dead lamb in her. Shirt off, I set about getting a hand in far enough to feel for legs and a head. They slid apart in the mucus and came out in putrefied, stinking bits. The ewe groaned encouragement, but as I went back in to check for any sign of a twin, her groans were drowned out by the sound of Tom throwing up. I ran back to the farm for penicillin, and after a day or two of touch-and-go the ewe survived. It was my first farming success. The failures elbow themselves into the memory, too. A ratching old Herdwick with multiple fleeces that had escaped over the walls at every gather for at least three years, but had still managed to creep back onto the farm to get mated every autumn. Queenie, my foxy red collie, found her in a corner of low-hung woodland with three wild, healthy lambs one, two and three years old. She was being eaten alive by maggots that had crawled from her tail through those welcoming fleeces. We dosed her and tried to bring her back, but she died and the youngest lamb died beside her.

On an October day of freezing fog, we headed out onto Wasdale Common. Five farmers, twelve dogs, me and a tape recorder. It was a stupid day to do the autumn gather, but bad weather had already delayed it a fortnight. We were going to round up the sheep on the mountain, the hefted flocks of Herdwicks and Swaledales that had wandered the common grazings out to Glade How all summer. By the time we'd done the 300 yards to the top of Wool Lonnen, the other farmers had disappeared into the mist, but we could still hear them whooping and cursing at dogs that yapped in the distance.

Tom, dressed in his standard fell farmer's uniform of Oxfam overcoat tied round with baler string, sat on a rock and had a cigarette. He said he would wait until the others had tired themselves out a bit. Or shut up, whichever was the sooner. The whooping faded, and Tom clicked a finger and whispered to his dog, Rob.

'Hwayby.' That's all he said.

We sat chatting for maybe twenty minutes until a gentle thrumming echoed through the grey and shifting clag, which formed into ghostly grey faces and then a flock of perhaps 200 sheep with Rob bobbing and weaving behind them. As the dog drew level with us, he looked over his shoulder and made to go back.

'Summat's stuck.' Tom picked up his crook, and we trudged up the hill to where the rolling common falls sharply away into the valley of the River Bleng. All the while, Rob kept running back to us and then ahead again leading the way.

We looked over the cliff edge where Rob was sitting, and on a ledge perhaps ten feet below us a Herdwick stood in front of a heap of droppings facing a licked and polished rock face. Tom, fully equipped for rock climbing in flapping, sodden coat and wellies, clambered down and pushed the sheep off. It turned in the air and landed twenty feet below on the springy fleece of its back. It lay still for a moment, then scrambled to its feet and began devouring Blengdale.

I'm not sure if that old Herdwick outlived Tom or not, but that morning in the mist was the image that came back most vividly to me when Tom died. He'd been ill for a year with cancer of the throat which came and went. But that may have been wishful thinking. Eventually, they carved out his voice-box.

'Kinder if they'd snipped off the tackle,' he scribbled on his notepad. 'Edna says I haven't needed that for a bit.' But neither disease nor attempted cure could stop Tom the raconteur. He became a master of sign language, and the moment of biro scribbling to a punch line just seemed to improve his sense of timing.

The beginning of the end came in the Bengarth farmyard. Tom had a coughing fit and all that came was blood. A handkerchief full and then a shirt front full. We rushed him to hospital in Whitehaven, where he was told they could keep him alive pumping blood in at one end while it continued to leak out at the other. The leak was inoperable.

The following day (the day before Christmas Eve as it happens), the family, complete with adopted son, was summoned. The young doctor who met us was in tears, but we could hear nurses laughing at Tom's notepad jokes in the room next door. Tom had decided to die.

I was called in first.

Scribble. 'What you looking so fucking miserable about?

Silence.

Scribble. '? ? ?'

'Because I'm fucking sad that you're going to die.'

Scribble. 'Well I'm not. I've had a good run.'

Silence. Filling eyes.

Scribble. 'Thanks.'

And then we got down to business. Tom had already written

down the funeral instructions. He wanted to be cremated. He wanted the cheapest coffin I could lay my hands on – cardboard preferably. Once he was in it, he wanted me to drive him to the crematorium in the farm van. No pricey hearse. No mourners, not even family. Wait two months and have a memorial service in the tiny church at Netherwasdale. And in a drawer in the bureau at Bengarth there was £400 to put behind the bar of the Strands Hotel that day to have a proper wake. He'd like a picture of himself behind the bar so people could raise a glass to his memory. Then, once all that was out of the way, I could spread his ashes on the crag overlooking Bengarth – so he could keep an eye on the buggers.

I suspected at the time that there might be rules about cardboard coffins decanted out of farm vans. I knew I couldn't tell the Purdham family they weren't welcome at the funeral. But it wasn't the moment to mention these things. The other sons – Tom, Jack and Dennis – joined us, and we talked about the price of sheep, the weather. Anything normal. Father Tom was tiring. He'd already refused blood transfusions. We all shook his hand as if we were taking leave at the end of an afternoon at Broughton Auction. He hadn't lost his firm grip.

Scribble. But more laboriously this time. 'Send the women in. They'll want to grieve.'

Edna and their daughters Connie and Margaret trooped in, and as I walked away the visiting carol singers were getting their scribbled instructions. 'While Shepherds Watched Their Flocks by Night' echoed down the long corridor to the lift.

During the recording of *The Shepherd's Tale* Tom had once said to me, 'Anyone who's seen the mother love of a common animal has got to believe in something.' I wish I'd remembered on that December afternoon. But on the way home from the hospital, I kept the tears back by remembering happy, sunny times with Tom. He was at his cantankerous best when we worked together on another programme called *The Allotment Show* for BBC 2. Part of Bengarth farm was turned into an allotment where we kept ducks and chickens, pigs and rabbits. Tom would organise the livestock. When I saw how many trips he'd made and how far he'd had to go to lay hands on such rare creatures as ducks, I realised why the farming industry was in such a parlous state.

One day I went with him to buy another endangered species – hens. I knew they were available from a farm down the road but, no, we would go to Longridge Auction in Lancashire. Longridge is a leftover from the age of Dickens. You could buy anything from a disassembled house to a guinea pig. People offer for sale a single pot plant or a garden rake without a handle. It's probably subsidised by the local Social Services Department. We stood about as everything from donkey harnesses to dolly tubs went under the hammer. Then we got to the hens. The first half-dozen in a cardboard box. I made my bid. £1. Someone else was bidding against me. The price went to £6. At this point the auctioneer halted proceedings, and said that he was sure I'd arrived with the man in the flat cap who was standing next to me. Were we sure we wanted to be bidding against each other? Tom slunk off to the cafe, and I got the overpriced hens.

Rabbits were another source of friction. Tom had insisted that breeding rabbits for meat was a perfectly sensible thing to do on an allotment. He knew someone who knew someone else who was a neighbour of someone who was an expert on rabbits. Eventually, three very handsome New Zealand rabbits arrived – two does and a buck. They were going to breed like – well – rabbits. They didn't. They seemed to be trying but nothing happened. It became a matter of some embarrassment to Tom. I'm sure he was going out at night and drawing them diagrams. As recording day got closer, Tom started to say that perhaps rabbits weren't suitable for allotments after all. The night before the OB truck was due, the rabbits mysteriously escaped. At which point they started to breed. There were wild white rabbits at Bengarth for years.

We recorded *The Allotment Show* – minus rabbits – at Bengarth on the hottest Lakeland day I ever remember. The Manchester outside broadcast truck we were using was old enough to remember Ally Pally, and its engineering manager had to spend the entire afternoon spraying it with a hosepipe to keep the temperature inside at a level which wouldn't blow its safety switches. Even so, 'Slippers' Farrington, the director, reckoned he'd lost a stone. Tom thought it had probably done him good.

That night we sat around the barbecue watching the sky over Wastwater Screes go deep purple and sent along to the village pub for further supplies. During the party, Tom said to me quietly that he reckoned he was buggered. Within ten minutes he was dancing and clattering his shepherd's boots, striking sparks into the night as he'd always done.

Tom's memorial service was crammed to the doors. The graveyard was full of cheery neighbours. It was a happy afternoon and in the Strands later a wildly drunken one. Tom stepped out of his portrait and strode the room. At one point, late on that evening, I passed a bemused American visitor who was shouting down the public phone and then holding out the handset towards the raucous singing in the room next door.

'Ahm a telling yer. It's a fooneral.'

A few days later, I rescued Tom's ashes from under the car seat and walked out in low sunshine to the crag overlooking the farm. I scattered them and said a rather self-conscious prayer. As I turned away, there were a few splatters of rain from a blackening cloud that crept over my shoulder. By the time I'd run the hundred yards to the roadside gate, I was soaked. The passing motorist must have wondered why a drenched man carrying a funerary urn was shouting at the sky.

'You old sod, you just have to have the last word.'

CHAPTER FIFTEEN
ARTOOR

Shortly after Tom died, *Farming Outlook* was killed off by Tyne Tees. I thought for a while that my connection with agricultural broadcasting was probably done for. I'd reckoned without Artoor.

For the best part of thirty years Arthur Anderson ran BBC Scotland's farming programme, *Landward*. When he heard of the demise of *Farming Outlook*, he invited me to join his team. In later years he used to say from that moment his expenses budget was never quite the same again. We worked together, on and off, until he was inconsiderate enough to retire. (I think the expenses budget ran out slightly earlier.)

I should explain the 'Artoor'. Arthur was fascinated by Eastern Europe and made many programmes there. More to the point, his Scottish regard for the etiquette of hospitality meant he drank many toasts there. From Moscow to Vladivostok, Bucharest to Gdansk, glasses would be drained to the continuing success of 'Scotchland', 'Breetish Brawncastik' and their plenipotentiary, 'Artoor'. Fortunately, his training on claret at his home in Auchenblae stood him in good stead, and he could generally walk from the room unaided. Unlike some of his hosts.

Artoor's proudest broadcasting boast was that he could find a story about Scottish farmers in any corner of the world, no matter how remote. Papua New Guinea was probably his greatest achievement. When I was working with him we found them in Newfoundland, Romania, Czechoslovakia and Poland. There Arthur discovered a remote township called Szkocja up near the Russian border, where lived an ancient farmer. He claimed to be descended from a chap called Burns, and said he was the last survivor of the immigrants who'd come from Scotland to work the land there in the eighteenth century. Mr Boorma was half-blind and wholly disillusioned with post-communist Poland. His farm was a vision of the mediaeval world. Sagging, half-roofed buildings surrounded a yard knee-high in disintegrating wooden carts and weeds. Mangy pigs were barred up in most of the buildings, scampering through their slurry and fighting over the food Mr Boorma's stocky daughter was tipping among the mess. We sat on a broken sledge in the middle of the yard, and the old farmer told me that in the good old, red old days he knew exactly how much he'd get for his pigs each month. Now the new-fangled almost market economy was breeding chaos. Gorbachev and Walesa should have been chhhk – a mime of knife across the throat. What the place really needed was another dose of Stalinism. Yes, a few people had suffered, but it had all been exaggerated by politicians who wanted a subdued Russia, and at least the price of pigs was under control then.

Mr Boorma's ancestors had been brought from Ayrshire by General Ludwik Pac, who'd gone on an agricultural Grand Tour and studied farming techniques in Scotland in the 1750s. Forty or fifty Scottish farmers and agricultural labourers made the long journey to the general's remote Dowspuda estate and never went home.

We found them in an overgrown graveyard walled into the middle of a vast arable field. Among the intertwined brambles and saplings were Armstrongs and Jardines, Douglases and

Scotts under rough-hewn memorials that carried messages of homesickness and longing. Almost as poignant were the deeds and contracts they'd signed all those years ago which we found in the regional archives. Some were signed in a flowing copperplate, others with a rough mark. Here were whole lives delineated by the number of loads of firewood they were allowed each year, what acreage of turnips they must grow, how many cattle they should keep. Volume after dusty volume of the bits and pieces of a Scottish community in a foreign land. Those documents would have been remarkable if they'd survived in the National Archives at Kew. In a broken-down building in a back street in Suwalki, they were extraordinary.

Suwalki was a three-horse, one-street frontier town, once an armaments staging post on the road to Mother Russia. We were told its street had been specially widened to allow tank transporters and ammunition lorries to pass. Its population wore depression as others wear an overcoat. Drunks shambled through the sparse traffic (the tank transporters and ammunition trucks having long gone). Old women in ragged black dragged themselves to half-empty shops. The hotel was the most modern building in town, three or four storeys of half-rendered concrete, but it could have been thrown up anytime from the 1930s to the 1970s. Its receptionist was of indeterminate years, too, and as hard and as badly made up as the hotel's facade. No, we couldn't see the rooms until we'd paid. In full. In hard currency. Artoor quibbled but soon realised the folly of such a course. He paid.

'Which way is the bar?'

'This way – and closed.'

'Restaurant?'

'Other way and open tomorrow.'

'Are there any other restaurants in town?'

'Open yesterday.'

She was voraciously counting the dollars for a fourth time as we headed for the lift. It thundered into life like a heavy engineering factory at the start of a shift, and had a metal plate screwed to the wall with thirty paragraphs of operating instructions. We were shaken to a halt in a pitch-black corridor, along which we navigated by Braille until we found our respective billets. They were hardly worth the effort. Seedy, stains of indefinable substances on the cracked plaster walls, and a naked light bulb throwing long shadows across the threadbare carpet. In caricature of a thousand and one Soviet travellers' tales, there was no toilet paper and no plug in the bath.

Later, at a shop which had a single can of Coca-Cola for display purposes only, we managed to rustle up some bread and greasy sausage, which we ate ostentatiously in the closed hotel restaurant. This little act of defiance obviously struck a chord with the waitress, who was on duty even though the restaurant was shut. She brought us a knife to share between the five of us, and then, realising she'd demonstrated weakness in the presence of capitalist interlopers, retreated to her position by the kitchen door where she glowered for the rest of the evening.

When we left the next morning, the half-rendered receptionist told us to make sure we left the bath plugs. Artoor had to be restrained.

To illustrate our story of the eighteenth-century Scots settlers, we wanted to film scenes of horse-powered agriculture. At one point on the long drive across northern Poland, we spotted a chap working a horse-drawn plough. Jan Ostrowski, our Polish cameraman from Northumberland, jumped out and offered him a couple of dollars if we could film him. He was happy to oblige, and when we'd gone he obviously got on his mobile phone to tip off his mates in the next few villages to put their tractors away and dust off the horse. Round every corner there were scenes of eighteenth-century life. Farmers relearning the art of driving a horse and cart while holding out a hand for dollar bills.

We had no such problems on our film trip to Romania the following year. In Romania it still is the eighteenth century. To ring the changes, we were following not a Scottish farmer but a Scottish agricultural machinery salesman this time. Tempted by the prospect of Romania perhaps getting into the European Community club, he was trying to set up a joint venture with the management of a failed tractor factory in Brasov.

The main works having gone bust, the few remaining engineers were scratching a living by making illicit spare parts for Ladas. Their machine shop was the sort of place where health and safety inspectors should be sent to restore their sense of perspective. Thundering lathes with not a safety guard to be seen. Noise levels that could have awakened the profoundly dead, let alone the profoundly deaf. And in a corner the half-completed potato harvester that was going to revolutionise Romanian agriculture. We were taken on a conducted tour of its chains and screens, invited to marvel at its cogs and riddles. This was the future and it was here. What hadn't materialised yet was the ability of any farmer in Romania to be able to afford to buy it. In fact, it was about as useful as two other giant and revolutionary machines that were rusting in the factory's back lot. Half combine harvester on steroids, half Bond movie, they were designed to clean out river beds. There was never any chance of them working, but as the designer happened to be called Ceausescu they got made anyway. The machinery salesman from Perthshire had inexplicably turned down the chance of buying them at a knock-down price.

Our filming trip to Romania took place a couple of years after the Ceausescus had been stood against a wall and shot, but the stage set they'd built in Bucharest and against which they played out the tragi-comedy of their dictatorship was as they left it. Boulevards of buildings in the imperial style constructed of cheap poured concrete and with no innards. A national theatre with no stage; a national library with no books. And skulking over it all was the monstrous Palace of the People, so big it could house the entire, unwanted Romany population of Romania. It was built on such a scale that it can apparently be seen from outer space.

I asked our contact at the Agriculture Ministry where Ceausescu and his wife were buried, and was pointed in the direction of a tatty municipal cemetery in one of the poorest suburbs of Bucharest. Originally he'd been buried in an unmarked grave, which was later sarcastically decorated with a black cross made from two welded lengths of scaffold pole. But then the Communist Party of Romania put up a florid memorial complete with a photograph showing the once Father of the Nation. When I asked the cemetery attendant where the grave was, he claimed not to know, but the comings and goings gave it away. That and the fact it was the only grave in the place sporting a florist's shop illuminated by several dozen candles. Poor people were coming to pray at the Ceausescu shrine. Like Mr Boorma in Poland, they were obviously, worryingly hankering for a strong man and guaranteed pig prices. When they saw me watching them, they scurried away into the shadows of the trees.

Later that day I drove north out of Bucharest, eventually shaking off the lingering cloud of industrial smog and the trail of battered chemical pipelines that lined the road. Soon the grim tower blocks were dropping out of sight, too – the urban prison camps into which Ceaucescu had forced the rural poor in a futile attempt to prove that Romania was an industrialised nation. And stretching ahead was a fertile and underdeveloped land that I'd been told was capable of providing a quarter of the agricultural production needed by an expanded Europe. In a field by the road a few children – no more than ten or eleven years old – were harvesting maize by hand. They bundled it and stacked it on an ancient long wooden cart drawn by a patiently dozing horse. The sun was setting and the pale leaves of the standing crop sparkled orange and gold. The children were laughing at the antics of the little girl with a pitchfork balanced on top of the load. It was a glorious, hopeful moment; a tiny, certain heartbeat in the corner of a landscape that seemed to stretch forever.

CHAPTER SIXTEEN
WAINWRIGHT

Landscapes closer to home, landscapes real and of the imagination were going to be the backdrop to my working life for the next few years. A BBC producer, Richard Else, had asked me to meet a fellwalker called Alfred Wainwright. I vaguely knew about him. He was the author of a series of idiosyncratic guides to the Lakeland fells. But in legend he was a grumpy, unattractive and reclusive man. He liked animals better than people, so they said. Oh, joy.

But if proof were needed that legends exist to conceal the truth, Alfred Wainwright provides it. From our very first filming day together, we got on well. He wasn't easy. The programmes were made despite him in many ways. But he was a man who knew the mountains of Lakeland better than anyone else apart from the fell shepherds. And he knew how to communicate that knowledge in a way that has inspired tens of thousands of people to be brave enough to make the exploration for themselves.

The sadness of my time with Wainwright was that I only knew him as an old man. The series made with him charted his decline. He died before the fifth series was finished. But there was still a bit of Jack the Lad trying to get out that day on Pen-y-gent when we first turned up with a crew to commit Wainwright to film. He'd come with a script, which wasn't a good start. We would walk down from the summit to Horton in Ribblesdale, chatting about his fondness for these limestone country landscapes as we went. But, crucially, I wouldn't know who he was until someone came up to him in the car park at the end of the walk and said, 'Good to see you, AW.' I would realise at that moment I was in the great man's presence, exclaim, 'Not THE AW?' and ask him to sign my book. As I told Richard at the time, that dénouement would have needed Olivier or, at the very least, Branagh to carry it off.

On the way down the hill, I tried every ruse I could think of to encourage AW to talk about himself. They all failed. Eventually, I tried the full frontal assault.

'What gave you the idea to write the first of the *Pictorial Guides*?'

Ominous, brooding silence. Gurgle from pipe. 'You can't ask me that because you don't know who I am yet.'

Then he smiled his Jack the Lad smile, and I realised that the script he'd done for us was probably a joke. At least, I think it was a joke.

There would be moments like that in the filming of every programme. I often wish Richard had been brave enough to put some of them into the final edit. It would have been cult viewing. But in a way it was. Wainwright's fans had waited a long time for this. For decades, he'd been the ghost on the hill. By the time one of his guides was published, he was away exploring some other remote corner of the fells. There were sightings as of the great white whale. People would gather at a remote mountain pass because rumour had it that Wainwright was travelling that way. Of course, he never showed. But now, here he was on the telly each week at 7.30, and this time he couldn't escape. He was the fellwalker in captivity.

He had appeared on television once before. He'd been tricked into turning up for some sort of meeting in

Manchester. When he came through the door, he found himself in a television studio in the full glare of the lights being interviewed by a gushing presenter. If he'd stumbled accidentally into a pit of snakes, he couldn't have found it a more slithering experience.

So, it's not surprising he was cagey when he started making the programmes with us. When he'd done his books, he'd had total control. Because they were handwritten and hand-drawn, there wasn't even the chance of a typesetting error. But when it came to television, he was putting himself into somebody else's hands. His way of coping with it was to operate a Wainwright ration book system. Each day he would arrive with a quota of stories and descriptions. When he'd used them up, he would suggest it was time he went home. That might be at 10.30 in the morning. Betty Wainwright would come to our rescue and suggest kindly but firmly that AW was only joking. He wasn't. But when Betty spoke, Wainwright acquiesced. He stayed but he said very little for the rest of the day. Instead he spent the hours looking out at imagined landscapes that his failing eyesight could no longer bring into sharp focus while occasionally giving a long, drawn out sigh. When it got to about 3.30 (earlier on Saturdays when he needed to get back to hear the Blackburn Rovers result), he would fold himself into Betty's tiny car and head for Coronation Street. He was a brave man. Anyone who was prepared to be a passenger with Betty deserved a medal. And I'm not saying anything about my friend Betty that I haven't said to her face, usually when she was doing a seventeen-point turn to get out of a thirty-acre field.

Talking of which, fields and the footpaths through them were a regular source of disgruntlement between Alfred Wainwright and the farmers of Lakeland. In his *Pictorial Guides* AW publicised public rights of way. The farmers for their part were sick of inconsiderate walkers who damaged walls, left gates open, and let their dogs loose among the livestock. You can see why the relationship could be a bit abrasive. While we were filming *Wainwright's Lakeland*, we took AW to the print works in Kendal where there was a Wainwright cottage industry, a squad who did nothing else but print and bind Wainwright books. It was only half a mile from where he lived, but he'd never bothered to go to see it. We happened to coincide with a group of farmers who were being given a tour of the factory. One of them peeled away from the group and said, 'You're that Wainwright fella, aren't you?'

Wainwright puffed on his pipe and pretended he was a printing press that was on fire. Even with his dicky eyesight, he could obviously spot a disgruntled farmer at some distance.

'Aye well, in yer book that deals with my farm you tell people to walk through a couple of my fields and turn right at the green gate.'

The smoke thickened.

'Well, I've sorted you out. I've painted the bugger black.'

I saw AW redden slightly through the smoke.

If the legends about Wainwright's *Pictorial Guides* were true, the farmer probably wouldn't have been troubled. It's said they were never intended for publication, but were just a personal aide-mémoire to remind AW of great days on the hill, when his legs would no longer take him there. That may have been the case with his experimental attempts at a first volume, but by the time he got into his stride, he knew they were too good to grace just one bookshelf. He was still amazed when they started to sell. By the time I was filming with him, he'd already sold a million copies. It must be going on two million by now. As his biographer, Hunter Davies, used to say, he'd done it with no advertising, no press releases, no PR advisers. Word of mouth alone sold them. Eat your heart out, Jeffrey Archer.

I never did discover why Wainwright made the mistake of calling his books guides. Guides are poor things. I've written guides. Any fool can write a guidebook. And it certainly wasn't because he was self-effacing about his work. He knew they were good, these crafted works of travelogue mixed with philosophy and journalism and occasional poetry. His interpretation of the Lake District – one of the great European landscapes – is still unrivalled. Much later, I took on the job of Chairman of the Cumbria Tourist Board. When in the wake of the foot and mouth outbreak we were trying to rebuild the area's tourism industry, I went back to the Wainwright books. I realised that they were the perfect works of reference about sustainable use of a fragile landscape.

In the years following Wainwright's death in 1991, I made several programmes in his memory. They were the beginning of a long collaboration with David Powell-Thompson – the headmaster from the first scene of this book – who had eventually made enough trips across the school playground with soil trickling from his trouser legs and had completed his escape tunnel from the education service. David became researcher, and between us we recreated for television Wainwright's first expedition through the Lakeland mountains, which we called the *Wainwright Memorial Walk*. AW had devised it by poring over Bartholomew maps on the floor of his back bedroom in Blackburn. It was to be a bold adventure during the Whitsun holidays in 1931 that he'd share with his mates in the Blackburn Borough Treasurer's office. He didn't know the mountains then and created a 102-mile, six-day walk that the SAS might have welcomed as a training challenge. It was utterly unachievable by office-bound Treasurer's assistants. One of Wainwright's days involved something like seventeen miles of hard walking followed by a trip to the summit of Blencathra after tea. They didn't manage it. To make sure others could, we spread the journey over eleven days – a walk that takes in all the major summits of central Lakeland, giving glimpses into most of the valleys and, weather permitting, most of the major lakes.

Emboldened by having pulled that one off, I suggested we should try the tougher companion volume. A walk through the lonely and often trackless mountains round the rim of Lakeland that Wainwright missed out of that first expedition. The result was *Wainwright's Remote Lakeland*. The summits may not have been as big, but laid end to end it produced a 190-mile walk with 40,000 feet of ascent, an Everest-and-a-half to be accomplished in fourteen days, starting and finishing at Penrith. We filmed it one autumn and were warmed, chilled and drenched in equal measure. Our several soaked attempts to climb Grisedale Pike have left me with chronic rising damp. But it was immense fun, and the little team that made those programmes still works together for three or four months every year making walking programmes across the north of England and southern Scotland. David and I are joined by Polish, rabid Europhobe cameraman Jan Ostrowski and sound recordist Terry Black, who gets to look more and more like Mr Pastry as the projects fly by. As the years go on, the flying becomes more like stumbling but what the hell.

Wainwright himself went on his final trip to Haystacks in 1991, his ashes carried up by Betty to become a bit of grit in a walker's boot, dear reader.

We'd been making a programme with him when he was taken ill. Much of it had already been filmed, and perhaps because he knew he was close to hanging up his boots, AW was unusually forthcoming about the hardships of his early years. It was as if he was trying to set at least a bit of the record straight about why he could be difficult, introverted and, at times, harsh. He told us about his father, who was an itinerant stonemason – more itinerant than stonemason and, more frequently still, drunk. He told us of his long-suffering mother of blessed memory and of the strange mores of back-to-back, terraced row Blackburn. AW was born with startlingly red hair (one of his nicknames was Red in later life); because nobody else in the family had red hair, he said he remembered as a baby being hidden in a drawer when visitors called.

But I think what startled me more than anything else Wainwright told me that day was that he wanted to visit his favourite patch of grass in the whole world one last time. The view wasn't much to write home about. It wasn't in Borrowdale or on Haystacks or at Wasdale Head. It was the centre circle at Ewood Park, the home of Blackburn Rovers Football Club. We took him there to the ground where he was one of the founder members of the supporters club. He stood misty eyed, sighed his trademark sigh, and seemed to be as close to heaven as an old fellwalker could be.

CHAPTER SEVENTEEN
GQT

You find me in a gloomy tin shed. For four days I've been entombed in the grey and soulless halls of the National Exhibition Centre at Birmingham, the stage turn for the Gardeners' World Live exhibition. Twice daily 500 or so visitors – keener I suspect to take the weight off their aching feet than to catch a glimpse of the stars of Radio 4 – have been cramming into what's known euphemistically as the BBC Celebrity Theatre. They are there to watch the cast of one of the world's longest running broadcast programmes grapple with the perennial problems of voracious slugs, wisterias that won't flower, and why it is that garden centres sell plants whose life expectancy is precisely the same as the time it takes you to get them home. *Gardeners' Question Time* is in full cry.

'I always watches Charlie Dimmock and wants my garden made over.'

The questioner in the front row seems to be sweating slightly as the image of Charlie's tee shirt rises into his limited field of consciousness. As gently as possible, chairman-cum-care worker, I translate the blather into something approaching an answerable question, and get shot of it in the direction of Nigel Colborn, John Cushnie and Bob Flowerdew.

Nigel wisely resists the temptation to do his quite excellent dirty old man impersonation, and instead is merely objectionable in spades about garden decking. John, who in life has very similar views, decides that on air the more pressing imperative is to disagree with Nigel, and so argues that decking is the greatest horticultural advance since Capability Brown was given his first trowel. Bob Flowerdew, the champion of organic – i.e. slow, laborious and pest-ridden – gardening embarks on a more Calvinist, philosophical point about the benefits to the soul of being forced to wait to see your garden mature.

'No, I doesn't want manure . . . don't like manure . . .'

We realise that the man in the front row has come awake again, having started to nod off twenty seconds into the answers when he realised that:

(a) Charlie Dimmock wasn't on the panel,
(b) he didn't know who was on the panel, and
(c) nobody on the panel was wearing a tee shirt with no bra.

I was tempted to suggest that Nigel Colborn in a tee shirt and no bra was not a pretty sight but thought better of it. The producer would just have cut it out for fear of offending one of those Radio 4 listeners who insist that the pictures are better on the wireless.

Bob the evangelist wasn't to be beaten by an inadequate with coprophobia. No fear of excrement has ever bothered him. We're treated to a concordance of composting – packing it, firing it up with recycled beer and cider, fondling it, heating it, running it through one's fingers and savouring it. He doesn't go quite as far as Geoffrey Smith, who used to say that properly made compost is so delightful you could eat it in sandwiches, but he does enough to send the man in the front row off into the hall to continue his lonely quest for Charlie laying paving slabs.

Discretion being the better part of composting, I move on to the next question.

'Joan Hammond from the Lake District. Our garden is at 1,200 feet, very exposed to the prevailing winds, and with about an inch and a half of poor soil. We also have an invasion of bracken and problems with marauding sheep. Could the panel suggest some shrubs which will give colour and scent all the year round?'

She stops short of asking for the shrubs to have edible berries, aphrodisiac qualities and an ability to scare off the neighbour's cat. But *Gardeners' Question Time* is firmly rooted in faith. Its audience believes that the members of the panel merely have to lay hands on a problem for it to be miraculously solved. Gardeners on the telly may have sex appeal or boyish good looks but, because of that, they're obviously fallible. Feet of clay. In GQT reside the high priests of horticulture, handing down their advice on tablets of York stone from their ethereal abode in the Elysian fields of the Home Service. Even though it doesn't sound like it at times.

'You don't want much.' A grunt from Cushnie accompanied by an echoing and devilish laugh from Flowerdew, and the questioner accepts the gentle rebuke as a sinner in the confessional. The lady from sheep and bracken country is then treated to a horticultural sermon by Archdeacon Colborn in which a cavalcade of shrubs appear and disappear in quick succession as if they're the prizes on the *Generation Game* conveyor belt. All there for the planting, so long as she remembers the wealth of cultural advice that the panel offers with each one of them and says her Hail Marys before committing them to the poor earth of Lakeland.

I should explain that I was several thousand questions in by this stage, having been confirmed in 1994 as the seventh chairman of one of the longest running broadcast programmes in the world. I'd inherited the rather perished wellies previously occupied by the likes of Franklin Engelmann, Freddie Grisewood, Michael Barratt and the programme's founder, Bob Stead. He devised and chaired GQT's forerunner – *How Does Your Garden Grow?* – in 1947 as a radical six-week experiment. In an age of scrupulously scripted radio, he was going to let ordinary people loose with the microphone. The first recording was at a pub in Ashton-under-Lyne. It was memorable because of an old chap who insisted on playing his cornet as he thought he'd come to a recording of the Wilfred Pickles programme *Have a Go*.

The early chairmen all had a jolly sight easier baptism than I did. For some months in 1992 the gardeners of Middle England had been fuming in their conservatories about what the BBC was planning to do to their favourite programme. They feared that Sunday lunchtimes were never going to be the same again.

BBC producers generally didn't like having to work on GQT. They regarded their stint on it as doing porridge. It didn't allow their creative juices to flow. They were bored by it and couldn't change it, and anyhow the regular panel tended to act like an autocratic board of directors rather than the bunch of insecure freelances they really were. Michael Green, then Controller of Radio 4, decided to give the programme to an independent producer who would be charged with doing a bit of gentle modernisation and freelance pest control.

Compost heap hit fan. The *Daily Mail* hadn't been so incensed since President Nasser took over the Suez Canal. Britain's best-loved gardening programme was going to be changed out of all recognition in an attempt to attract a yoof audience. There was going to be music and comedy and *dumbing down*. It was the first time the BBC had to get to grips with that phrase, and the experience was probably instructive given that in the years since then it's been applied to every programme in the *Radio Times*. There was constant speculation about who would be the new chairman. Prince Charles, David Jenkins the turbulent Bishop of Durham, Ken Livingstone and Roddy Llewellyn were all hinted at by one correspondent or another. No doubt the young gardeners of Britain, taking time off from their house music and extramarital sex to do a spot of pricking out, could hardly wait.

Instead they ended up with me. The *Guardian* described me as 'an old hand', the *Express* as 'a green fingered traditionalist'. There was the unmistakable sound of millions of young people turning up the CD player and jumping back into bed. It goes without saying that I was delighted to get the job. Freelances are always delighted to get the job. What I wasn't prepared for was the article and colour photograph on the front page of the *Daily Telegraph* telling everybody else I'd got the job. The article itself was unremarkable, merely hammering another fence post into the BBC's supposed plans to attract a younger audience by describing me as 'a safe pair of hands.' The photograph was nothing special either, except that it had to be taken in a neighbour's garden because mine looked such a bloody mess.

It was the fact that there *was* an article and colour photograph of GQT's new chairman on the front page of the *Daily Telegraph* that was troubling. Forget the crisis that was enveloping Russia, ignore the chaos in the Middle East, don't give a thought to the swelling international tides of refugees, poverty and despair. Front page news is a bearded chap nobody's ever heard of taking over a gardening programme on the wireless. So all's well with the world then.

At least it was for a week until I was rung up by Michael Green. He told me I'd better brush up on my horticultural Latin because I no longer had a panel of gardening experts.

They'd defected to Classic FM. The leader of the revolt who marched his troops across the Green Line was Dr Stefan Buczacki, who was apparently miffed at not being offered the chairman's job himself. He'd been the stand-in chairman since Clay Jones retired because of ill health, and obviously expected to keep the seat he'd been warming. For those who don't remember him, Stefan is a bearded, bow-tied, bantam cock of a chap about whom nobody is ambivalent. You know they say that you should never trust a man with a beard because he's obviously got something to hide. I've never entirely agreed with that proposition for obvious reasons. But the conjunction of beard and bow tie with a measure of pomposity thrown in is a fearsome combination.

There was an irony in all this because some years earlier, when I was producing *The Allotment Show* for BBC 2, I gave Stefan one of his first broadcasting breaks. We included a feature each week about new scientific developments in horticulture, and a rather more reticent and self-effacing Buczacki explained to us the possibilities of genetic manipulation of crops. As I remember from this distance, he suggested that one day it might be possible to have a plant that produced potatoes underground and strawberries on top. At the end of the recording, he shook my hand and thanked me for taking an interest in his work and making the recording so easy for him. I bet that was a handshake he regretted in 1994.

War had been declared. Michael Green at Radio 4 was incandescent, his remarks about Stefan and the 'traitors' unreportable. His opposite number at Classic FM, Michael Bukht, did what he could to increase the embarrassment by announcing a substantial sponsorship deal for his newly acquired programme, courtesy of the Cheltenham and Gloucester. (Some years later this gave Trevor Taylor, the new independent producer of *Gardeners' Question Time*, a ready-made response to a listener who asked what Stefan was doing now. 'Last heard of working for a building society,' was the reply.)

But we still had the problem of getting GQT back on the air. Michael Green had junked the half-dozen programmes the old team had already recorded. We needed a show for the following Sunday. Every stop and string was pulled. The concert studio at Broadcasting House in Manchester was booked. An audience of several hundred gardeners was gathered in from across the north of England. The *Daily Mail* was invited to send a photographer and reporter. A high-risk strategy given that, at the time, I was going to be answering all the questions.

But it's a measure of Stefan's popularity in the hothouse world of horticultural broadcasting that we had so little trouble finding a top quality team who were delighted to join the programme now he'd gone. Geoffrey Smith came back, having earlier given up the show because he couldn't stand the temperament of its interim chairman. (Mind you, I eventually rubbed Geoff up the wrong way, too, by being cocky and inconsiderate.) Pippa Greenwood brought her amused and unrivalled expertise in garden pests and diseases from *Gardeners' World* on television, and the plantsman Adrian Bloom added a gentle certainty to the proceedings even though he didn't make it into the final pool of regular panellists. In the weeks that followed, we were joined by an already overworked Geoff Hamilton, who dibbled us into his impossible schedule because he believed that GQT shouldn't be damaged by 'a bunch of back-stabbing primadonnas'.

Listening to the stories that started to emerge about the ancien regime – tales of childish tantrums and humourless, domineering chairmanship, of unforgivable rudeness to the nervous secretaries of little local gardening societies, and the extraordinary demand that questions had to be submitted weeks in advance so the team could mug up the answers – a less than bucolic picture emerged. But it wasn't all bad. Apparently, during Ken Ford's time as producer and chairman, the team used to stay in downmarket bed and breakfast houses and claim the full overnight allowances. The savings went into a kitty to help pay for fertility treatment for one of the secretaries. Practical propagation in action.

Generally, though, the atmosphere was poisonous. I might have been terrified by the prospect of facing the *Daily Mail*'s reporter, but equally I was mightily relieved that the old lot had gone.

Except for Fred Downham. He was quintessential *Gardeners' Question Time*, an old working gardener who, like Fred Loads and Bill Sowerbutts before him, brought a whiff of well-rotted manure and a relish of bastard trenching to his performance. I'd first met him when I auditioned for the programme in London. He was part of the makeshift panel that the aspiring chairmen had to keep in order. He was also terrified that Stefan would find out he'd been fraternising with the enemy. He would have been an asset to the programme and told me he was looking forward to being part of it. Instead, he shuffled off behind Stefan to Classic FM.

The first recording with the new team in February 1994 went better than we could have hoped. Like the nervous cast of some off-off-Broadway show, we scoured the early editions to see if it was thumbs up or curtains.

'They tiptoed, not through the tulips, but through trepidation,' began the *Daily Mail* article next morning. 'The setting for the pre-recording of Sunday's show was unpromising – a cavernous theatre with rows of banked seats rather than the traditional cosy village hall. The whispered conversations were of the show's past chairmen, the legendary Clay Jones and the professorial Dr Stefan Buczacki.'

Oh, dear. But then it got better. Modesty should prevent me from including the next bit. But I'm not that modest.

'Bearded Mr Robson is nothing if not professional. He bounded into the cauldron and kept his audience spellbound with what amounted to a stand-up routine of which any comic would have been proud.

'It was that warm up spot – in which he pleaded "be gentle" after referring to "the odd column inch" the upheaval had caused – which nurtured, every bit as much as the wit and wisdom that followed, the success of the first edition of *Gardeners' Question Time* Mark Two.'

We'd got away with it. Which goes to prove that throwing yourself on the audience's mercy is an invaluable part of the broadcaster's armoury. It was also helpful that neither the *Daily Mail* nor the audience knew me from Adam.

But then we had to set about producing fifty-two programmes a year, keeping our regular weekly audience of two million or so – many of whom had been listening to *Gardeners' Question Time* for decades – and at the same time trying to introduce some gentle innovations which might attract a new generation of listeners. The potting shed was one of these. I invented it in a throwaway remark at the start of one of our regular correspondence programmes in which we answer questions listeners send in by post. At the time we used to record these shows in whatever village hall we happened to be visiting the previous week. But the idea caught on. People began to write in to ask where the potting shed was and if it would be possible to visit it.

The producer, Trevor Taylor, a one-time BBC staffer who worked on the *Today* programme, was already conjuring with the idea of the programme having its own garden. After protracted negotiations with Radio 4, he got agreement and did a deal with Sparsholt College near Winchester, which was prepared to let us lay out a garden in a corner of their grounds – complete with a potting shed cleverly kitted out to function as a recording studio. It's been up and running for some years, but the legacy of my early fictional shed persists. We still get letters from listeners saying that they know the potting shed isn't real, but congratulate us on how well we carry off the deception. And this is despite the fact that four or five thousand people a year pop their heads round its door when they join us for the programme's annual summer garden party.

GQT is a travelling circus. We clock up a huge mileage each year to make recordings all over the UK and two or three times a year in Europe. In fact, we have a big European audience. Many thousands of expats tune in their long wave radios each Sunday or get the programme by satellite. An old lady who turned up at one of our recordings in Spain told me that she spent half an hour every Sunday afternoon on top of the wardrobe in her spare bedroom because that was the only place in her house where she could pick up a long wave signal. Nigel Colborn immediately jumped in to demonstrate the breadth of his knowledge when he offered her a guaranteed cure for cramp.

But mostly we're in village halls, school halls, golf clubs and community centres from Sutherland to Somerset, East Anglia to the Isle of Man and Ireland. We record two shows a night, and if you listen carefully you should be able to spot which ones we've recorded back to back. You'll hear a programme in which we're guests of a school in Windermere, and a couple of months later you'll hear one featuring questions from gardeners in Cumbria. Economies of scale. But more to the point, it further demonstrates the skill of the panellists. Not only are they hearing the question for the first time when it's asked at the recording – no mugging up for the experts these days – but they're also having to work out that the programme they're recording in

September won't hit the air until mid-November. This, of course, has a considerable bearing on the advice they give.

After all these years of doing the programme, I still marvel at the team's ability to cope with what Trevor and I throw at them. Together we sift the questions that come from the audience in the hall – mainly to make sure that we don't get slugs, moles in lawns, non-flowering wisteria, vine weevil and mare's-tail in every programme. But all Trevor and I know is what's written on the card. We generally don't see any samples the questioners have concealed about their person. All we can do is take the questions at face value, which occasionally leads to some unexpected exchanges.

Question: 'As you can see from this leaf sample, we have a problem with our pear tree, which is embarrassing because it's in the front garden of the Pear Tree Hotel.'

Answer: 'It's more embarrassing than you think because it isn't a pear tree.'

Question: 'Is there anything I can use to stop caterpillars doing this sort of damage to my brassicas? (Cabbage leaf with nibbled edges appears from handbag.)

Answer: 'Those caterpillars are pigeons.' (Panellist goes seque into rendering of Tom Lehrer's 'Poisoning Pigeons in the Park', and after the round of applause I have to make it clear that he was only joking, just in case any militant member of the Royal Society for the Protection of Birds should happen to be listening. There being no Royal Society for the Protection of Caterpillars, we can splat, squelch or poison them at will.)

The audience in the hall has a huge impact on the quality of the programme. The best audiences turn up determined to have a good night out. The panellists oblige with their tried and tested blend of solid horticultural advice and good humour. Occasionally, though, we find ourselves facing an audience that is determined to glower. They sit there stony-faced, challenging us to make them laugh. There will be an occasional groan when the names of the questioners are read out, and you realise that for the rest of the evening our hosts are going to be acting out the squabbles and petty jealousies that make their gardening club such a joyous place to be.

Mind you, it's easy to misread an audience. I remember once doing a couple of programmes in – well, let's just say somewhere on the Norfolk coast to spare their blushes. It was one of those seaside towns with a reputation of being God's waiting room. As I looked out over the audience, I was reminded of what one of the earlier chairmen told me when I got the job. 'There'll be places you go to', he said, 'where you and the panel will be the only people in the room with your own teeth and hair.' That night in Norfolk the audience warm-up raised not a titter. By the time we got to the third question, a number of people in the front rows were fast asleep. The air was thick with the twittering of badly tuned hearing aids. They were not the best programmes we'd ever made. But the following week a letter arrived from the organiser thanking us for our efforts and saying it was the best night out they'd had in years. One had to wonder how audiences in that sleepy seaside town reacted on a bad night.

There was a postscript to that story. As we were drowning our sorrows that evening in copious quantities of Kingfisher beer in the local Indian restaurant, our outside broadcast van was broken into and all our microphones stolen. Presumably by the local chapter of hell's grannies.

After most recordings there's the dreaded raffle. Dreaded because it's amazing how many things can go wrong with a raffle. On our visit to a Women's Institute somewhere in Ireland, the lady organising the raffle was so keen not to miss any of the recordings that she put the counterfoils into the drum the night before – not knowing how many books of tickets she would sell. I seem to remember there were seventeen prizes that night, and we had to draw 164 tickets before we found all the winners. And then there was the raffle organiser who didn't notice she was selling two books of blue tickets with exactly the same numbers. We had quite a punch-up over who'd won the bottle of whisky that night. On another occasion most of the prizes were carried off by the committee. I'm not sure if that gardening club is still going.

But there are plenty left. When Trevor Taylor's company took over the programme, he inherited a list of 2,500 outstanding invitations. *Gardeners' Question Time* had already been going for almost fifty years, and here we had another fifty years' supply of venues. Trevor sensibly wrote to them all to ask if they were still alive (of course, he put it rather more tactfully than that). Most replied that they'd still like the programme to come, and would we please hurry up because they weren't sure they could hang on much longer. We went to one society that had sent its initial invitation thirty-three years earlier. The lady who wrote it was in the audience and as sharp as Bob Flowerdew's secateurs.

One of Trevor's gentle developments of the programme was to find more unusual locations for our recordings. We went to a prison and to a London Underground station. Our grandest trip was aboard the Swan Hellenic cruise ship *Minerva* on her maiden voyage round the Mediterranean. Our most widely reported was a recording at a nudist camp. The team was given the option of baring all and joining in the healthy, goose-pimply fun, but we all decided that being several shades paler than our audience might detract from the sense of occasion. In other words, we chickened out. Trevor suggested that if we weren't going to strip off, we should at least dress down. I did my bit by wearing a two-piece rather than a three-piece suit. It was a jolly afternoon with much merriment about the dangers of nudists cutting thistles and backing into gooseberry bushes, and we got a round of applause every time the audience sat down.

Very occasionally, I get a letter from a stalwart listener who complains that there's too much humour in the programme these days. That we're too easy-going, that we don't treat gardening with the seriousness it deserves. I generally write back and remind them of the way it was in the glory days. On the panel then were Professor Alan Gemmell, Fred Loads and Bill Sowerbutts, all under the stern eye of chairman Ken Ford. During one recording there was a question about blue pansies or some such, and Fred Loads rattled on about them for a couple of minutes. When he'd finished there was a pause, and Bill Sowerbutts said, 'Nay, I know nowt about them either.' Not a lot has changed.

CHAPTER EIGHTEEN
ON MANOEUVRES

The year I took over as chairman of *Gardeners' Question Time* – 1994 – was probably the busiest I've ever had, because as well as a weekly gardening programme and the routine calendar of state events, the Outside Broadcast department also went to war.

A string of Second World War fiftieth anniversaries meant I was on parade for some months. In June we remembered D-Day in a week of coverage that stretched the technical resources of the BBC to the limit. Unfortunately, we were led not by Dwight D. Eisenhower but by Philip S. Gilbert.

There was never a meeting of minds between Mr Gilbert and me, which may colour the comments that follow. The new head of television events programmes prided himself on his grasp of detail. He would spend long hours ensuring that the optimum number of photocopiers would be available to the production team on location. But when faced with a real problem that needed him to sort out some high-ranking army officer or a flunky of the Royal Household, he could always think of a way of being otherwise engaged. His producers grumbled and sank in a sea of paperwork. Philip loved paperwork. Recently, I came across a copy of one of his missives to the D-Day producers. It runs to more than 300 photocopied pages of military memos and other such assembled bumf, and contains much valuable information such as who would be responsible for providing the rubbish skips on Southsea Common at Portsmouth and the fact that enemy forces were not expected to put in an appearance.

Just as well. We had quite enough on our plate trying to make sense of Philip's trendy new style of outside broadcasts. Ever since the ill-fated Royal Wedding, OBs had become the place where the House of Windsor met Breakfast TV. Somebody, somewhere had decided that the audience no longer had the attention span to be able to keep up with the plot of a long broadcast. So each programme had to be broken up into bite-sized morsels, and had to have its clutch of self-styled experts, pundits, fashion consultants, gossipers and armchair generals. All were paraded on a sofa with a view in a sort of garden shed on steroids built to overlook one of the main event sites.

The D-Day celebrations were presented by John Tusa, one-time head of the BBC World Service and eventually of the Barbican Centre in London. His shed was on the Normandy beaches at Arromanche. John is a consummate broadcaster who has a knack of being able to take the most complex history or politics and make it instantly understandable in a few well-crafted and apparently effortless sentences. His frustration at having to ringmaster a cast of flannellers was equally apparent.

My job was easier, commentating on the two opening events at Portsmouth – Beating Retreat and an open-air service which, between them, would let us tell the story of the gathering of hundreds of thousands of troops and more than 5,000 ships in preparation for the invasion of Europe. For the commentator these set-piece military spectacles are the easiest sort of outside broadcast. They tell a thrilling tale, and there's music galore during which you can collect your thoughts.

For many viewers the very worst commentator's sin is to talk over the music – even if that music is provided by one of the B-list military bands that are but a fractured quaver away from the Boys' Brigade on a bad day. The aficionados still want to hear it in all its horror. On the occasions when my words have strayed over the opening bars, I've had the letters exploding with anger and underlined in green ink to prove it. I got a lot of those the year I commentated on Beating Retreat at Horse Guards Parade in London when the band from a regiment it would be unkind to identify was so dreadful that Mike Begg, the producer, told me to talk over as much of the performance as possible. I was naming the Horse Guards' pigeons by the end of the fifty minutes and my local postman had a hernia, but at least I prevented Berlioz and Sousa from having to rotate in their graves.

There was no such problem that year in Portsmouth. The five bands from Britain, Canada and America were good enough to make the Queen Mother beam, and Her Majesty's demeanour was a very good barometer of the quality of martial music. My job was made easier still by having a reporter on hand to do occasional interviews with people attending the event, who all said what a lovely day it was, and what a lovely time they were having, and how lovely the Queen Mother looked. But the reporter, Jill Dando, made it all seem less superficial than that in her lovely, gentle, unflustered way.

The following day on Southsea Common I was introducing the Archbishop of Canterbury, who was to lead a drumhead service. Drums and the flags of the wartime allies were arranged into a temporary altar as they would have been on many a distant battlefield. Church services are particularly tricky for the commentator because talking over the prayers is a worse sin than talking over the music. But archbishops love pauses and filling overly long pauses is what the commentator is paid to do. So you have to get to know the archbishoply body language and keep talking until the precise moment he begins to stir from his reverie. You also have to know how to finish the sentence quickly while sounding as if you're working at the episcopal pace. Sawn-off sentences are another serious commentary failure.

After the service there was the ceremonial – thirty warships from seven nations, all taking veterans back to the beaches; a flotilla including *Canberra*, *QE2* and the biggest aircraft carrier in the world, *USS George Washington*. All reviewed from the deck of the royal yacht by the Queen, President Clinton and the heads of state or their representatives from the fourteen wartime allies. This is when the commentator really earns his crust. Moving ships about is an imprecise business. A manoeuvre could take five minutes or it could take fifteen, and you're expected to fill whatever it takes. Of course, you'll have done your research. You'll know all manner of details, some well known and some obscure, about what happened that nervous day in 1944. You'll have read what the BBC war correspondents said as they waited to sail with the armada to Normandy. But you'll probably need more. You'll know details of the ships, their armaments, their crews, their captains, their battle honours and their gross tonnages. After a battle with the Buckingham Palace press office, you'll have discovered the most highly sensitive detail of the day – what the Queen is wearing.

And still more. You'll have squirreled away the number of people who can sit down to eat on the royal yacht, what President Clinton had for lunch, the weight of the anchor, the precise configuration of the yacht's propulsion system, and how far it can sail on a full tank. Of course, if you get this far down the list, you're in trouble.

The relationship between commentator and director is crucial. Odd as it may seem, quite a lot of directors rarely listen to what the commentator is saying and go their own sweet way, cutting to whatever shot takes their fancy. The inevitable end result is that the commentator is made to look a prat. At one ceremonial OB we had agreed I'd take the lead when it came to naming the royal guests. I was picking my way through the line-up of minor European royalty as we waited for the Queen to arrive, and proudly rattling off identifications of people who probably weren't even recognisable in their own countries.

'. . . and to her left the Princess of Liechtenstein . . .'

At this point the director cut to a severely bearded gentleman who bore a striking resemblance to Prince Michael of Kent.

The broadcast carried on in this vein for some minutes, with the director hanging me out to dry through the royal houses of Norway, Monaco and Belgium. Eventually, I leaned on the microphone mute key and suggested down the line to the director in the scanner that he was successfully encouraging viewers to believe that the crowned heads of Europe suffered not only from haemophilia and scrofula but also from transvestism. There was a magisterial silence from the director, and the vision mixer cut up a shot of Prince Claus of the Netherlands, saying with some glee, 'I suppose this will be Santa Claus, then.' I didn't rise to the bait.

But it was unprofessional of me to have had that exchange with the director in the first place, because the most burnished golden rule of commentary boxes is that you never say anything you wouldn't want to go out on air. It's just too easy to hit the wrong button or for some technical gremlin to send your jolly, unflattering throwaway lines to the airwaves. In fairness, that was probably what caused David Dimbleby to be heard chatting during the two minute silence one Remembrance Sunday. Yes, I know it's taken me a lot of pages to set the record straight, but better late than never.

Fortunately for my favourite OB director, Mike Begg, sound feeds from the outside broadcast scanner went no further than the commentator, the cameramen and the often bemused staff at Television Centre. When he was directing a royal OB, the air as well as the blood was blue. He suffered fools not at all, and it didn't matter a bit if the fool in question happened to be in line for a throne. I've heard the parentage of all manner of princes and senior army officers being called into question while at the same time I've been introducing them on air as charismatic, brave or talented.

But when Begg wasn't berating the cast – and he tended to see minor royalty as bit players in his production – he was at least listening to the commentary and helping to smooth its flow wherever he could. He was a staunch monarchist and seemed to know as much about the inner workings of the Royal Household as the Lord Chamberlain. He didn't want the Queen let down by the supporting cast. Particularly if the performer in question was a ham-fisted commentator who'd just misinterpreted an arcane piece of royal protocol. Between cutting to camera seventeen and checking that the rain-lashed operator of camera thirty-two was still alive on a tower crane 200 feet above the Mall, he would be explaining to me in forensic detail why the particular saddle cloth I'd failed to identify correctly was important. And more than that, he would offer me another shot of it in twenty seconds or so, by which time he hoped I'd have got my facts straight so I could correct the error and not make his contacts at the palace think he was in charge of amateur night out.

'Steady, camera ten, we're covering the Queen's procession, not the bloody 4.30 at Market Rasen.'

Up comes shot of saddle cloth on cue and I duly correct my error.

'Better, but you still didn't mention the embroidered badge of the Coldstream Guards. No, camera four, try to find some soldiers that look as if they come from the British army, not the bloody Panamanian militia.'

How he kept it all in his head I don't know, because – on this OB as on so many others – the first thing he'd done when he arrived in the scanner that morning was to throw away the camera script running to maybe eighty closely typed pages with every camera shot listed. A script he now thought would cramp his style. In other words, we would all be flying by the seat of our pants again.

Mike had been doing that all the way through his BBC career, and many people said it was a miracle he'd ever made it to producer. Mind you, I never heard anyone brave enough to say it in his presence. Mike started as a stage manager, and on one occasion was sent to work on a live outside broadcast from the Royal Opera House, Covent Garden. As it was an evening performance the bars of Covent Garden beckoned in the late afternoon. He went walkabout with his drinking companion, another stage manager called Ronnie Pantlin, who looked rather like a well-oiled Scottish laird just in from the stalking. Before the drinking started, they scoured the local flower shops to buy the armfuls of blooms that would be thrown down from the gantry during the final curtain calls. The flowers did a considerable pub crawl before being taken back to the theatre, and our two heroes made their way unsteadily to a position high above the stage. They dozed and were awakened by the final applause, at which point they jumped to their feet and began to throw the flowers. Unfortunately, there was a lighting bar above their heads which guillotined each bloom. The flowers stayed on the gantry and the stalks rained onto the stage – to the great amusement of the audience who, Mike suggested afterwards, took it as an entirely appropriate comment on the quality of the performance.

I was flying by the seat of my pants in Mr Begg's company later in 1994, but this time in Arnhem when we commemorated the fiftieth anniversary of Operation Market

Garden, the plan to drop thousands of parachutists behind enemy lines to secure vital bridges across rivers and canals in Holland. If we could have held them, the allied army would have been able to push on quickly into the lowlands of Germany, skirting the defences of the Seigfried Line. It should have ended the war by Christmas 1944, but as we know the bridge at Arnhem was the bridge too far. Operation Market Garden failed, but in its failure it created many heroes.

And for Mike it was the heroes that mattered. The ceremonial, the spectacular camera shots created at vast expense, and the musical accompaniment were just set dressing. The war graves cemetery at Oosterbeek near Arnhem was a stage on which the heroes of the glorious attempt could be celebrated. They were the stars of the show. I've never seen Mike angrier than the day a commentator, who'd watched some interviews with survivors of a particular battle, suggested he could paraphrase what they said and get the same information across in a quarter of the time. By the time Begg had finished explaining that the only heroic thing the commentator had ever done was to avoid being run over by a bus on his way to the stage door of some poxy Scottish theatre where he was to act badly in a second-rate production of a play which should never have been written, the BBC Club bar in Kensington House and the commentator were entirely silent.

In the weeks before the Arnhem broadcast, Mike assembled a cast of veterans and local people who'd helped them during the battle and in the aftermath of the defeat. He recorded their stories and illustrated them with archive film. On the day of the anniversary service, Prince Charles and all manner of important people were at Oosterbeek. But the heart and soul of our programme was being able to zoom slowly in through the vast gathering and find a man or woman, nameless in the crowd, standing with head bowed, whose story we could bring to life. A widow who, as a young girl, had saved the lives of countless British soldiers by persuading her parents to hide them in their cellar. An old soldier who had fought with Lieutenant-Colonel John Frost in the vain attempt to hold the Arnhem Bridge. Eventually down to a handful of men in two badly damaged houses at the foot of the bridge, they sent a final radio message, 'Out of Ammo. God save the King,' and surrendered.

The people Mike had chosen spoke with a mixture of passion and forbearance that no jobbing commentator could bring to those memories. Listening to them speak and seeing those gentle people among a sea of faces, each one of which held other, unspoken recollections, was a humbling experience. I hope it was for the people watching the broadcast.

This technique of mixing live OBs with prerecorded inserts was also a high-risk strategy. We were gambling that the event would run to time. If it didn't we were in trouble, with a tape machine broadcasting one of the moving personal stories while at the same time the service of remembrance was starting or Prince Charles was half-way through his walkabout. What made it even riskier at Arnhem was that we were relying on the Dutch television service to supply us with pictures. They were broadcasting it live, too (without tape inserts), and they weren't going to delay things for the BBC. The night before the broadcast I suggested to Mike that we'd better have a fall-back position in case things got terribly out of kilter. His answer was typically decisive.

'We already have one. You.'

Mike generally did the interviews himself, because he didn't want the egos of jumped up reporters and commentators to get in the way of the real people. But a couple of years earlier – in a rare compliment I've got to say – he'd asked me to interview some of the survivors of the First World War for his programme *It'll Be All Over By Christmas*. We travelled to the fashionable little seaside town of Sidmouth in Devon to meet Captain G.B. Jameson, formerly of the Northumberland Hussars. He was ninety-nine years old. He was in the trenches at Christmas 1914 when British and German soldiers climbed out into no-man's-land, shook hands, sang Christmas carols and showed each other pictures of their families. He was very matter of fact about it.

'Yes, our people were wandering about on the top and talking. They were singing all sorts of carols. They weren't wanting to fight really, you know. They went through the motions, so to speak, but there was no real war going on. It was very quiet in that part of the world.'

It wasn't in G.B. Jameson's Sidmouth. We arrived at his flat at breakfast time to find him having his first glass of whisky of the day. We had to be quick about it in the interview department because he had places to go and things to do. Interview over, he donned his Biggles goggles and climbed aboard his invalid buggy. But this was no geriatric conveyance. By law it was limited to four miles an hour, but he had a mate who had a friend who'd managed to re-engineer the back axle so it did fifteen. Our cameraman manfully tried to keep up as we filmed him terrorising motorists on the way to a local hotel where he swam seven lengths of the pool each morning – the first three under water. He then retired to a local pub, where he had a hearty lunch and several pints before heading unsteadily home to ring the lady he was going to ask to marry him.

Mike and I, faced with intimations of inadequacy if not mortality, didn't say much on the way back to London.

CHAPTER NINETEEN
OUT OF TOWN

At the time of writing I've been a freelance for more than thirty years, and I've been lucky to have had a variety of broadcasting jobs unmatched by most proper broadcasters. As a result partly of incompetence and partly idleness, I somehow avoided the straitjacket of a career structure and steadfastly refused to be an expert or a specialist in anything. Putting a more positive spin on things, I've always maintained that being the outside broadcaster was a mission, not an accident. When people ask me what sort of broadcasting I specialise in, I tend to say that I'm the electronic equivalent of the jobbing plumber. (And as any electrician, joiner or bricklayer will tell you, the jobbing plumber only needs to know two things – water runs downhill and pay-day is Friday.) But despite having been one of the BBC's state occasion voices, the chairman of *Gardeners' Question Time* and all the rest of it, I know that in large areas of the north of England I'm going to be remembered not for my commentating skills or documentary-making excellence, but as that bearded chap who went walking with a cantankerous dog on a string. A dog that happens to talk.

It began as a one-off cheap and cheerful series for the BBC in Newcastle called *Out and About*. Ten years later, it's a cheap and even more cheerful series for ITV called *Out of Town*.

The BBC in the North East had changed out of all

recognition since the days when John Mapplebeck was holding his editorial meetings in the front bar of the Portland and producing two programmes a week. They had a new headquarters – known locally as the pink palace – which was the BBC's last major investment in regional broadcasting and which now stands half-empty, producing almost nothing but the local news.

Like so many gloomy corners of the Birtian empire, it had become a nest of political correctness. Sitting tightly on that nest was Olwen Hocking, the new head of centre, who spoke with her master's voice and whose jargon-rich memos gave boundless pleasure to true lovers of the English language. At one of our earliest meetings she suggested that my on-screen image would benefit from professional help. She happened to have an image consultant to hand, who looked me up and down and fiddled with her flip charts for a while before announcing that I was a purple person. On the table in front of me an identikit Robson was being assembled. New hairstyle, reshaped beard, clothes that disguised the shape I've been for twenty-odd years, and shoes, dainty shoes that would make me appear lighter on my feet.

'And what do you think of that?' said the head of images with a lavish, unveiling sort of motion.

'I think', said I, showing remarkable restraint, 'that it would make me look like a dickhead.'

'You mustn't mind Eric, he always speaks his mind,' said Olwen the diplomat, obviously aware that the image consultant's own image had changed from oleaginous to thunderous. As I clumped out in my brogues I heard her say, 'He's in denial you know, which is so, so often the case with men of a certain age.' I didn't wait to hear if Olwen agreed or not.

Quite what rush of blood to the head persuaded Olwen to let me loose on a walking programme I don't know, but I suspect it was something worthy, such as persuading people who were orthopaedically challenged to take more exercise. Either that or the great outdoors was the perfect place to lose someone with a five bob hairstyle and no dress sense.

The dog was an afterthought. At the time I had a Border Terrier pup called Raq. He was named after the dog that belonged to one of my broadcasting heroes – George Bramwell Evens, better known as Romany of the BBC. He was the world's first great natural history broadcaster, a middle-aged gentleman who pretended to go on country walks with two little girls called Muriel and Doris. Just imagine trying to get that past the BBC commissioning process today. Anyhow, his Raq was a spaniel that snuffled in hedge bottoms and put up the occasional pheasant. All snuffles and bird noises came from sound effects discs because the walks were actually done in a radio studio in Manchester. But Raq still became a star. When Bramwell Evens died, dozens of people wrote to the BBC offering his dog a home. Maybe having the Border Terrier on my walks wouldn't be such a bad idea after all.

The first time I took him out was a filthy day of steady, penetrating rain. He was tiny, just five or six months old, and he sat in the top of my rucksack, looking sodden and disapproving of the rain-lashed views over my shoulder. If you don't know Border Terriers, I should explain that they're born looking like grumpy old men.

But we got fan mail. To be more precise, the dog got fan mail. And so it's been for more than ten years. During each series the little fragrant letters start to appear with pictures of cats and puppies and woofy little messages from Jasper and Maximilian and Andre. The letters are often signed with a paw print. They tell tales of chasing rabbits and suggest walks that one dog thinks another dog will like. Research doesn't come any cheaper than that.

The string was deliberate. When I was farming I always had a length of baler twine in my pocket to tie up everything from farm gates to the Land Rover exhaust. It was also the perfect disposable lead. Not all dog owners agree. I've had very sniffy letters suggesting that having a dog on a string is demeaning to the poor animal, that he'll end up with psychological problems. And viewers send leads. Posh ones, woven ones, extending leads, training leads. More than seventy at the last count. As I say to people with dogs that we meet along the way, Raq's the only dog in the north of England that gets a new lead every day. Anyhow, the string lead is his instantly recognisable trademark. That and the fact that he's cantankerous, opinionated and deeply politically incorrect.

I can't remember when he started to talk, but I think it was after we moved to ITV, the BBC having decided they'd had quite enough opinionated walking programmes. In those days the opinions were mine. But there are some thoughts that the programme presenter would find it difficult to express while maintaining his impartiality. I may think that certain parts of Sunderland would benefit immensely from the attentions of a firm of demolition contractors, but shouldn't say it. It may be apparent that a particular landowner who's giving us grief for walking across his estate is a grasping fascist, but grasping fascists tend to have high-priced lawyers. It's surely self-evident that wind farms are an economic and technological nonsense, sustainable only if the government stuffs their owners' mouths with money, but slack-brained environmentalists hail them as the answer to all our prayers.

I can't say any of those things in the programme but the dog can. He gets away with it. The good people of Sunderland say what a cheeky little chap he is, fascist landowners tend to get on better with dogs than people anyway, and not even the most rabid Friend of the Earth has yet managed to blame global warming on the activities of irresponsible Border Terriers. And as the icing on the cake, because the dog spends much of his time being rude about me, I also get the sympathy vote.

So off we trot for three months every year to spread offence and merriment round the north of England and southern Scotland. The format is simple. Find a place that offers good walking in an interesting landscape, and then unearth the obscure footnotes of history that bring the place to life. Dipsomaniac duchesses and secret canals, forgotten railways and wayside gibbets, the mad, the bad and the beautiful ladies who were walled up in the west wing. There's no shortage of them. Every hamlet has a list of half-remembered characters that would make two or three programmes.

Some of the characters we dug up were so extraordinarily larger than life that we gave them a series of their own. There was Maharajah Duleep Singh, the last child king of the Punjab who, having been deposed by the British and forced to hand over his jewels – which happened to include the Kohinoor diamond – naturally became a favourite of Queen Victoria. For a while he lived near Whitby in a house where he entertained spies and revolutionaries in the hope that a Russian invasion of India would restore him to his throne. It's said that he built the long, straight road between Whitby and Sandsend to exercise his elephants. That bit is total baloney, but it's still too good a story to miss.

And there was the strange tale of Trebitsch Lincoln, who began life as a petty crook in Hungary. In short order he became a missionary, an Anglican curate, a spy and an oil-speculating confidence trickster before being elected Liberal Member of Parliament for Darlington. He was a German agent during both World Wars, managed to con Lloyd George, J. Edgar Hoover and Himmler, and ended up as a Buddhist abbot in Shanghai. There's a CV to make people sit up, count their fingers and make sure their wallet is still in their pocket.

One of the joys of filming *Out of Town* and some of its spin-off programmes was the access they gave us to places normally closed to the public – the anoraked classes, as one duchess of our acquaintance used to call the fee-paying visitors to her stately home. As it's me saying this, not the dog, I'd better make it clear this wasn't the dipsomaniac duchess of earlier report. The really interesting bits of all castles and stately homes are the areas on the other side of the rope. We spent one very happy summer scrambling through the attics and cellars of grand houses all over the north of England in the company of jolly owners whose various shades of madness seemed to be in direct proportion to how much of their home had been eaten by dry rot.

I remember standing on the crumbling battlements of a castle up near the England–Scotland border, listening to the dry rot creeping up the stairs and to its owner saying that, if the conditions were just right, you could look down from the tower and see King Henry VIII and his entire court walking through the gardens. But as he'd just finished telling me that the spectre of a mediaeval warrior lived in the building, jumping through walls and sometimes attacking his son who, because of his SAS training, managed to beat him off, that didn't seem out of the ordinary at all. After we'd heard that there were also happy ghosts in the castle who laboured away helping him with the restoration programme, we decided we'd had a spirit too many (and he probably had, too) and began to pack up the film gear. Terry Black, the sound recordist, was making conversation in an offhand sort of way.

'So does madness run in the family?'

To which the owner thought for a moment and said, 'It comes and goes.'

Terry can get away with questions like that. If the rest of us tried it, we'd be slung out on our ear. Maybe it's his Essex accent. People hear the Canvey Island drawl and assume he can't help it. Maybe it's his crumpled, grey haired, beaming habit. Whatever the reason, Terry is an asset. Nobody puts an interviewee at ease better. At the first sign of nervousness, Terry springs into action.

'Have you got another shirt?'

'Is it causing a problem with the microphone?'

'No, I just thought you wouldn't want to be seen in public wearing something like that.'

This exchange is particularly rich given that Terry is wearing a garish short-sleeved Caribbean kitsch number that may have passed muster on a cheap package holiday in Malaga, but is singularly out of place on a winter's afternoon in an academic's study in Durham.

Jan Ostrowski, the cameraman, is less rude and more serious as befits a man who once studied religious iconography. But he still has a finely tuned Polish sense of humour. For those of you unfamiliar with a Polish sense of humour, the punch line is invariably, 'If it wasn't for us you'd have been overrun by the Russians.'

And the final member of the team is the researcher David Powell-Thompson, who understands and appreciates the Polish sense of humour, being married to a statuesque lady of Polish extraction and living on the Cumberland coast, which, to my knowledge, has never been overrun by the Russians.

That's the squad: four men and a scruffy dog who criss-cross the northern hills in all weathers in search of secret places and hidden history. Weather is our burden and our delight. You'd imagine that the sensible time of year to make walking programmes would be the summer. Long filming days and golden light. But not a bit of it. Most series of *Out of Town* are commissioned in October or November to be delivered the following March. That's what passes for a commissioning editor's sense of humour. He sits in his cosy office all winter while we tramp the mountains through blizzard and downpour. That's the burden. The delight comes in thinking of 101 painful things to do to the commissioning editor as we trudge, heads down, rain streaming from our faces, across some God-forsaken moor in search of a waterfall that David assures us will look really spectacular in this abundant weather.

'We'll be the judge of that,' says Jan, stumbling into the mud again under the weight of his fifty-six-pound camera pack.

Terry, who's rearranging the black bin liner that's keeping the rain out of his sound gear while at the same time slaloming down a particularly greasy slope, shouts that he's never, EVER, going to do one of these bloody stupid walks again as long as he lives, which may not be more than a week because he's sure he's got pneumonia and trench foot. If I had a pound for every time I've heard him shout that on a God-forsaken moor, I'd be able to make the programme budget balance.

When we got there, the waterfall was almost as spectacular as the cloudburst that unleashed itself on us as we tried to film it. The dog turned to camera on cue and said that he was never, EVER, going to do one of these stupid walks again as long as he lived, which may not be more than a week because he was sure he had pneumonia and trench foot, and would anyone watching please ring the RSPCA.

'I don't think they look after sound recordists,' said Terry, reaching for his phone and ringing his wife Barbara, who is his ever-present help in trouble. Ever present because he spends about eight hours a day on the mobile to her – more if he hits the scotch in the hotel bar and rings her when he turns in and then falls asleep, leaving Barbara at home in Penrith shouting down a loudly snoring handset.

But one of the great successes of the series is that viewers just love watching us suffer. The most popular programmes are the ones when we're drenched and shivering. That more or less guarantees a big share of the audience, which gives you some idea of the levels of incipient sadism that lurk in the British viewing public.

Each series is slightly different. One year we did a world tour, travelling to such exotic places as New York, Van Dieman's Land, Hong Kong, Quebec and Moscow. And not one of these places is more than fifty miles from Newcastle. In another series we went in search of great film and television locations – the power station on Tyneside where part of *Alien 3* was shot, the beach at Bamburgh where some of *El Cid* was filmed. We strolled through the back of frame as an episode of *Last of the Summer Wine* was made in Yorkshire. Peter Sallis particularly liked the dog, and Terry said he thought I would make a very good Compo if I smartened myself up a bit. We climbed over the Hardknott Pass where Julie Walters had starred in *She'll Be Wearing Pink Pyjamas*. This was where their location catering van got stuck on a one-in-three hairpin bend and its chip fryers caught fire. And we mingled with the fans of *Heartbeat* who wander aimlessly about on summer Saturday afternoons in Goathland, the village on the North York Moors where the series is filmed, hoping to catch a glimpse of its stars. They were nowhere to be found, of course, and the fans had to make do with a dog on a string instead.

The year of the foot and mouth outbreak was a challenge given that most of the countryside was shut. But as the funeral pyres smouldered, we came up with alternative walks along abandoned railway lines, backstreet rambles through town history, and even an underground journey through the dripping tunnels of the Nenthead lead mines. As ever, the crew provided the black humour and the inspiration for the dog's worst excesses of grumbling and offensiveness. They became so much a part of the programme that they began to appear. Their off-camera remarks about the presenter's obvious lack of talent no longer hit the cutting room floor. When Terry's notorious meanness about radio mike batteries caused the sound to break up yet again (we're sure he warms them up in the oven to get another few minutes' life out of them), we carried on filming while he rummaged for another second-hand battery among the jumble of chocolate bars and mints that live in the dark recesses of his sound kit.

'It's amazing that we can get a signal from the moon but not across five yards of Lakeland footpath,' I grumbled.

'That's because Neil Armstrong knew how to PRO-JECT. If ever YOU learn to do it you might be a proper presenter some day, but in the meantime go take a giant leap for mankind.' Terry didn't actually say 'take a giant leap for mankind', and what he did say on that occasion had to be cut out.

One of the successes of *Out of Town* is that it treats the business of broadcasting with the same haughty lack of respect that it treats petty bureaucracies and official stupidities, the sending up of which are its stock-in-trade. For a decade the broadcasting companies have been laying off production staff, and replacing them with administrators whose principal aim in life is to think of ever more convoluted paper trails to keep themselves in the job that never existed in the first place. On one level that's fine and dandy. The fewer in-house producers there are, the more work is available for independent producers like us. But I swear I spend almost as much time filling in meaningless forms as I spend making programmes these days. For each programme I make, I have to fill in a diversity return which tells somebody, somewhere how many white, black, Asian, Chinese, mixed race, other non-white, disabled and over-55-year-old contributors appear. I have to break it all down into male and female, and say if they were portrayed in a neutral light, a positive light, a negative light or a mixture of all of those. Now, given that we interview people because they have a particular story to tell, not because of their colour or disability – and given that many of our interviewees would take serious exception to being asked if they're over 55 as a preamble to talking to them about their local village history – these forms are completely meaningless.

So, too, are the catch-all risk assessment forms that are another joyous reminder that a new series is on the way. By the time you've waded through innumerable pages of potential hazards that have precisely no relevance to the project you're about to make – nuclear threat, war zone, chemical attack – you begin to lose the will to live. In fact, the thought of a chemical attack begins to take on a certain old-fashioned charm. When I submitted a risk assessment for a particular programme that involved some high mountain walking, I filled in what I thought was the only relevant heading – extreme environments. When asked to give my assessment of the risk, I wrote (I thought remarkably honestly), 'Dangerous. If wet or in high winds, bloody dangerous.'

Wrong. The risk assessments lady berated me for not taking the vital project seriously. And what was I thinking about when I didn't fill in the section about electricity?

'What electricity?'

'You use lights.'

'Not often, because we're an outdoor programme, which by its very nature means that most people will be interviewed, er, outdoors.'

'But you can't rule out using lights in exceptional circumstances.'

'No.'

'And lights use electricity.'

'Even independent producers from Cumbria have given up using candles and carbide lamps.'

Withering look. 'All we're trying to do is make sure you and, more important, the people who work for you . . .'

I let that pass.

'. . . don't get electrocuted.'

'Our researcher's a fully qualified electrician.'

'And I'm a fully qualified risk assessment organiser.'

'But can you change a plug?' Pushing my luck has been a regular failing.

'What you're supposed to do . . .' icy now '. . . is to ask each interviewee to show you their home's electrical safety certificate before you do the interview. And also to point out the routes of emergency escape from their property in case there's a fire.'

Now call me an old fool who's out of touch with modern reality, but don't most houses have a front door and a back door (one of which our endangered film crew has just used)? And how many people do you know who have an electrical safety certificate? Even if they do have one, how many could lay their hands on it at short notice? Most interviewees are doing us a favour by giving freely of their time and expertise. The last thing they need is some wally asking them questions about the safety of their home while at the same time rearranging their furniture, using their highly dangerous electricity for their lights, and hoping for the offer of a cup of tea produced by boiling water in a kettle which, before operating, we'd have to check has been electrically safety tested in the past twelve months. By the time all risk aversion has been satisfied, the interviewee is a bundle of nerves, his wife has turned out so many drawers looking for the missing electrical safety certificate that she'll have to spring clean, and I've forgotten what we were going to interview the chap about anyway.

We head for the hills – Kentmere Pike in snow, Sharp Edge in a force seven, Striding Edge glistening with ice – where at least it's just bloody dangerous in an old-fashioned, unregulated sort of way. The dog grumbles the snow's deeper than he is, he's suffering from a bad attack of wind, and it's not only brass monkeys that suffer when certain nether regions are as close to the ice as his are. Jan has to tie himself to a rock to keep the camera steady in the gusting wind, and Terry reckons he's got third-degree hypothermia. Bliss. The only moaning we can hear is from the gale lashing about on the summit of Blencathra.

Fortunately, I've had another bolthole from television bureaucracy for some years – a company called Striding Edge. The original idea came from Richard Else, the producer of the BBC Wainwright series. Surely we could sell the programmes on VHS? We contacted the BBC to negotiate the rights and discovered that some bloke called Pegg from Kent had got there before us. I arranged to meet him in the unpromising surroundings of a bar on London's Victoria Station. From that first pint of overpriced warm bitter, we hit it off.

David Pegg is a marketing man by profession and Renaissance man by instinct. His talk of rough and dirty figures and P and L accounts is interspersed with titbits from his well-left-of-centre reading and an accompaniment of the most catholic taste in music it's possible to have. He introduced me to musicians that, on first hearing their names, I thought were diseases. But between us we created Striding Edge, a marketing company specialising in VHS and DVD productions about fell walking – and fell walking in the Lake District in particular.

The reason the company became a bolthole is that we make our own productions – the *Wainwright Memorial Walk* and *Wainwright's Remote Lakeland* and any number of 'Great Walks' in the Lake District, Scotland and the Yorkshire Dales. We make the programmes we want to make and sell them on to the telly afterwards – take them or leave them. They generally take them because nobody does fell walking programmes better, if I say so myself.

No, be fair, that's only the second boast in these pages.

Sadly, David's now retired from the company to spend more time with the builders who are pretending to restore a house for him in Italy. He's tried talking rough and dirty figures to them without success. Now he's going to play them some of his more extraordinary music. That'll do the trick.

CHAPTER TWENTY
END OF EMPIRE

We were bouncing in high winds between the washing-draped balconies of Kowloon City on the final approach to one of the most famous runways in the world – runway 13 of Hong Kong's old Kai Tak Airport. The British Airways flight from London, which a moment ago was apparently heading directly for a mountain, has made its stomach-hurling forty-seven-degree turn, surfed the tower blocks and clamped itself onto the tarmac, rushing towards the sea with every brake applied. Only one plane ever actually fell into the sea in Kai Tak's seventy-year history, but hundreds of thousands of white-knuckled passengers had a fleeting moment of doubt before their jumbo jet shook itself to a halt and lumbered away to the terminal.

As I'd left home in Wasdale two days earlier, one of the local fishermen at the pool by the bridge on the River Irt said he'd never forgive me if I gave away the empire. But that's exactly what this trip was all about – the handover of Britain's last major colony to the Chinese at the chimes of midnight on June 30th 1997.

It was a big deal for the outside broadcaster, working in a team that included Brian Hanrahan, who'd counted them all out and counted them all back in the Falklands. As Chris Patten, the last British Governor of Hong Kong, said later, 'You can only bring the empire to an end once.'

The omens weren't good. Hong Kong was about to be lashed by summer storms. The Chinese army was massing on the border, so it was said. There was even a rumour that the BBC team would make ideal hostages if the Chinese cut up rough. More immediately, the BBC engineers were trying to make the gear work and laying plans to keep the torrential rain out of the electrical circuits. We rehearsed what we could, which wasn't much, and prayed the forecasts were wrong – on all counts. The democracy movement in the colony was praying, too. One of their spokesmen said that bad weather through the hours of the handover would prove that the Chinese leadership didn't have the Mandate of Heaven, as he described it; that the return to China didn't have the blessing of the gods.

The gods had always been a bit sniffy about Britain's adventures in Hong Kong, and the colony has been a regular source of embarrassment for the British government. Opium, prostitution, corruption and gambling made a rich broth to be consumed by Britain's detractors. But the gods gave us a breather for Brian Hanrahan's broadcast. It seemed set fair as Chris Patten tearfully watched the Union Jack being hauled down for the last time at Government House. The organisers of the event tried very hard to make the folding up of the standard a moment of imperial dignity, but it still looked rather as if Mr Patten was taking away a set of folded curtains as a souvenir.

But then the gods got back into their stride for my first commentary on the twilight of empire. The very heavens wept (copyright Tom Fleming 1986) as British troops assembled at East Tamar on the Hong Kong harbourside for what was billed as the farewell event complete with fireworks. The Chinese put out a spoiler story saying that the British had never been very good with pyrotechnics, and that their £8 million display the following day would really show who was boss. Fireworks are difficult for commentators. Think of the inanities you hear at the average bonfire night display, and you get an idea of just how difficult. Once you've described one multi-coloured starburst, there's very little left to say about the twenty-third, which looks remarkably similar. That evening in Hong Kong I was helped by the fact that you could scarcely see the fireworks for the rain.

I was helped even more when Prince Charles tried to make his 'it's a far, far better thing we do' speech in a downpour the like of which had not been seen since the London Fire Brigade provided the showers for Ealing comedies. The rain poured from the peak of his cap so spectacularly that there were moments when it looked as if he was a talking waterfall. The sound of the cloudburst on the commentary box roof was so deafening that there were times when I couldn't be sure the waterfall was still talking.

But at least I had a commentary box. Poor Paul Reynolds, the Radio 4 commentator, was camped outside the television commentary box door. As the storm broke I invited him in, but too late. By then such notes as he'd prepared were so much papier-mâché. He soldiered on with immense professionalism, as did the sodden engineering crew who were keeping us on the air through cables and junction boxes displaying sparks and flashes that would have given a Chinese pyrotechnician something to think about.

We dripped off the air, and I then had five or six hours before I was back in the commentary box to cover the final departure of Hong Kong's British rulers. Five or six hours to get the notes into my head for what was scheduled to be a forty-minute broadcast. Easy. Except, as with the predictions of bad weather for the afternoon event, there had been whispers that things might not go entirely as planned.

On the face of it, the departure should have been as simple as can be. Prince Charles and ex-Governor Patten would board the royal yacht at Hong Kong harbourside, and after a bit of music and marching up and down, the ship would sail. Somewhere across Victoria Harbour it would disappear into the night heading for Manila, where the royals and politicians would take a plane home and the final curtain would come down on the centuries of imperial theatre.

We'd done what we could to make sure things would go as smoothly as possible. The captain of *Britannia* tested casting off the moorings several times, and reported back that he'd be able to get the old lady away from the quayside and into open water in about ten minutes. If the bad weather continued, she'd be obscured by the driving rain in another ten at the most. That meant we had twenty leisurely minutes for the final farewells and their musical accompaniment.

As it turned out, that was a serious underestimate. The royal party arrived on the dockside and the band of the Royal Marines struck up. Thousands of people thronged the dockyard perimeter. So far so good. But when the planned musical programme was finished, the handshakes were still going on. The band improvised. I improvised. Whatever Chris Patten had said in official speeches, he obviously didn't want to go. He shook hands with the entire staff of Government House and with anybody else who strayed within grasping distance, which looked as if it was half the population of Hong Kong.

By the time he and his daughters got to the companion way and started to board, we'd already been on air for half an hour, and the Pattens still didn't seem to want to break the imperial thread. They got emotional. The daughters sobbed. They waved for Britain. They then lined the rail and waved some more. Forty minutes. I didn't point it up in the commentary, but I'm sure we could hear the captain revving *Britannia's* engines in much the same way that taxi drivers do to get errant fares out of the pub.

Eventually the royal yacht slipped her lines and set off on what would be her very last official voyage. By this time I was dredging the stand-by information that would normally only have cluttered my sad memory rather than the viewer's. *Britannia* was the 75th royal yacht since the reign of Charles II. She was 44 years old, and had sailed 1,087,623 nautical miles on 696 royal visits overseas and 272 in home waters. She displaced 3,927 tonnes standard and 5,678 tonnes full. Her length was 109.7 metres at the keel, 115.8 metres at the waterline, and 125.6 metres overall. The beam was 16.7 metres. The mean draught was 5.2 metres, with a minimum draught of 4.8 metres. *Britannia* had a range of 3,675 nautical miles at 14 knots, 2,800 nautical miles at 20 knots.

No, I didn't use any of that. But it was touch and go. And did I mention that the weather had cleared slightly so we'd be able to see *Britannia* all the way across Victoria Harbour? We'd be on the air for at least another three-quarters of an hour. Fortunately for me (and the millions watching at home), the imperial history of Hong Kong and Victoria Harbour's part in it was considerably more fascinating than the displacement tonnage. Did you realize, for example, that Hong Kong was originally third choice for the mandarins of the Foreign Office? Lord Palmerston, the Foreign Secretary, had wanted Chusan, while his officials fancied setting up their Far Eastern base on Formosa. It was only the great, deep, defensible anchorage lying among the Hong Kong islands that persuaded them to change their minds. That and the fact somebody pointed out Formosa is bigger than Ireland and would be a tad difficult to defend. I think it was the mention of Ireland that swayed it.

But despite the delays, when *Britannia*'s lights eventually merged with the black horizon, it was quite a moving moment. I seem to remember that the commentary prose had turned close to mauve if not quite purple.

Some years later I read a speech that Chris Patten had made in America, during which he touched on those final moments of British rule. As they sailed away, his daughters were apparently throwing up over the side because it was a bit choppy. The next day, at sea, the royal yacht sailed through a great gathering of British capital ships while Prince Charles reviewed the fleet. (It was the last ever such review from a royal yacht because *Britannia* was about to be flogged off to become a tourist attraction in Leith Harbour of all places.) The Prince ticked off Mr Patten for not wearing a tie. On the approach to Manila they were greeted by the Philippines Navy, which fired a twenty-one gun salute with what turned out to be live rounds.

'Then,' he said, 'my wife, three daughters and I got into a plane and flew back to Heathrow with our luggage and came out of Terminal 3 and tried to get a taxi. That's how the British empire really ended.'

If only I'd known all that on the night, it would have perked up the commentary no end.

After the broadcast the BBC crew retired to its adopted watering hole in Wanchai. The Old China Hand in Lockhart Road was sandwiched between Suzie Wong bars that offered many varieties of exotic relaxation. After a hard day's imperial broadcasting, we settled instead for San Miguel lager and drank the place dry before dawn. There was much brave talk of what we'd do if the Chinese army burst in, but by three in the morning the general consensus was surrender.

The following lunchtime I went back for a hangover shift, and found that the old China hand I was sitting beside at the bar came from Holmrook, which is about three miles from where I live in the Lake District. It turned into a merry afternoon as the chap from home called up his various English drinking mates, who joined us in relays. He proudly introduced me as the only other chap in the whole of Hong Kong who knew that Holmrook existed. It was as if, in the nervous hours after the Chinese takeover, he needed the comfort of knowing that his other home was still there, still accessible.

After a marathon session of patriotic fervour, they eventually decanted me into a cab for the airport. I thanked them out loud for their alcoholic generosity as I sat on the plane listening to the very pukka captain calmly telling us it was going to be a particularly nasty and uncomfortable take-off because the mother of all electrical storms was crashing around us. I looked out of the window and saw a fork of lightning illuminate the Kowloon skyline, and the next thing I remember was waking up in the middle of the night somewhere over the Himalayas.

Just two months later I was again getting up in the middle of the night, but this time into a world that had gone mad. It was three in the morning in the Farmers Club just off London's Whitehall. When I looked out from my bedroom window, along towards the Ministry of Defence building, it was like the morning rush hour. Except that the people thronging the street were moving like sleepwalkers. Some were holding hands. A few of them carried lit candles.

It was September 6th, the day the world grieved itself to a standstill. The short walk through Horse Guards to the Mall was a strange experience. A modern city turned mediaeval with people praying and crying on street corners. A man drawing strange symbols in chalk on a pavement. And candles and flowers everywhere; armfuls of flowers which would eventually be strewn on the roadways in the path of the passing saintly martyr.

For a week, across the world there had been no news but the death of Diana, Princess of Wales. American TV audiences were living on British time. The suicide bombing of a shopping mall in Jerusalem scarcely made the papers. In India, mourning for Mother Theresa would have to wait. Even George Harrison's disparaging remarks about Oasis and the Spice Girls were scarcely reported.

I strolled along the Mall towards Buckingham Palace, and chatted to some of the people who'd camped out all night by the roadside to make sure they got the best view of the final earthly journey of 'The People's Princess'. Some had brought their children to experience what they felt sure was going to be one of the great moments of British history. Others were too overcome to talk, as if they were in the throes of a terrible, personal bereavement. Everywhere there were banners:

All America Mourns
3.5 Million Australians Are Sharing Your Grief
Farewell My Angel

And beneath the trees of the Mall there was a quiet, almost imperceptible sigh of sobbing.

The Princess Diana effect, as it came to be known, was very worrying. Here were gathered tens of thousands of people, many – probably most – of whom had voraciously consumed every bit of salacious tittle-tattle that the tabloid papers could throw at them about Diana's sexual exploits and medical abnormalities. Yet here they were at the first light of a September London morning preparing to canonise the same frail woman. Her death had been a tragedy, but so had much of her life. Her achievements as a mother and a champion of charitable causes would soon merit fewer column inches than the conspiracy theories about her death and whether or nor she really had been pregnant by Dodi Fayed. But this morning was a time for fairy tales. Diana as Cinderella with the glass slipper broken and the ugly sisters in the palace.

Of course, it wasn't my place to say these things quite so bluntly on the day of the funeral, being just one of fifteen commentators covering the proceedings for BBC Radio. An essay about press hypocrisy and mass hysteria might have sat uncomfortably amongst it all. But I mention these troublesome thoughts that surfaced on my stroll along the Mall on my way to the commentary box just to make the point that commentating is an imprecise craft. It may involve a sort of megalomania when you're let loose with an open microphone and a slab of airtime, but there are self-imposed boundaries not to be crossed. And the most important of those boundaries is the frontier of the land where personal opinion dwells.

My job on the morning of the funeral was to explain in more detail than would be needed for a television broadcast what was going on in front of me, and to reflect the atmosphere among the sombre crowds lining the route fifteen deep by that stage. The people listening to the broadcast would have to make up their own minds about the sincerity of those condolences from strangers. I would mention the array of floral tributes and quote some of the messages attached to them, but it would be up to the listeners to decide if they would write such things to a princess they had only ever seen in the papers or on television.

My station was in the Mall opposite the entrance to St James's Palace, where the royal princes would step into the procession behind the coffin. Prince Philip and Prince Charles flanked William and Harry and Earl Spencer. They looked neither to right nor to left. Philip the representative of a royal house that had been bitterly criticised in previous days for its harsh treatment of the princess. Charles, grey and drawn, the lightning rod for the crowd's antagonism. Earl Spencer, tight-lipped, head slightly bowed, seemed somehow lost. But how he would rise to the challenge when he gave his eulogy at the service in the Abbey. His criticisms of the press and paparazzi and the royal family itself brought the crowds to their feet in cheers of agreement and supportive applause.

William and Harry. Dignified, trained to the job but still no different from any other, ordinary sons who've had to follow their young mother's coffin. The card from twelve-year-old Harry, lying among the flowers on that coffin, simply said 'Mummy'. It made some of the more overblown messages of sympathy and togetherness strewn along the Mall seem even more out of place.

Many of the people crowded around the commentary box and perched on its scaffolding for a better view were listening to the proceedings on radio. There was an unnerving moment as the procession moved away past Marlborough House when I looked up and into the eyes of a woman whose nose was pressed to the perspex window of the box. Her radio was pressed to her ear, and she was mouthing my commentary back at me. She gave me a smile and a thumbs up, so I'd obviously pleased one of the three million people lining the route.

After I'd handed on to commentator six, I stepped out of the box and listened to the rest of the event on her wireless. It was a peculiar broadcast and a strange, muddled mix of voices, as if every outpost of the BBC Radio empire had felt the need to be represented. There were sports reporters and DJs, news presenters and interviewers. John Inverdale from the football department, Fergal Keane and Alan Little representing the foreign correspondents. Sue MacGregor from the *Today* programme, Nick Clarke from *The World at One*, and Chris Stuart and Simon Mayo providing the musical accompaniment. Hanging onto the reins of this carriage and fifteen were Jim Naughtie and his postillion Paul Reynolds. But as they were working out of Studio 1A at Broadcasting House that morning, at least Paul didn't have to commentate from a handful of papier-mâché.

After the service and when the hearse had gone by across its carpet of flowers, I walked with the dispersing crowds down towards Admiralty Arch and past the ivy-covered flint citadel on the edge of Horse Guards Parade. I bumped into a farming family from near Carlisle who'd come down especially for the funeral, but hoped to fit in a bit of sightseeing before they caught the train home.

'I've heard you doing all this Trooping the Colour stuff on the box so you'll be able to tell the kids what's what.'

Border Television viewers have always felt they have a claim on their local presenters. For a very pleasant half-hour the outside broadcaster became blue badge guide as we strolled around Horse Guards Parade. I told them many things they probably didn't even want to know about the buildings, the statues and the history of the most famous parade ground in the English-speaking world. All stuff I'd picked up over the years in preparation for untimely delays in state events that hadn't materialized. I thanked them for giving me the chance to use it at last – the location of Henry VIII's bear pit and real tennis court, the former Paymaster General's office that had its eighteenth-century façade moved from George Street in 1910, the mortar from Cadiz presented by the Spanish government in 1814, the barrel-vaulted Treasury Passage that leads through to Downing Street.

'And where are you when you're doing Trooping the Colour, then?'

They were obviously getting bored.

'In a garden shed up there on top of the Chancellor of the Exchequer's back garden wall.'

I drew the line at giving details of the vertical scaffold pipe that was the emergency toilet facilities.

'Is it really a garden shed?'

'Well, that makes it sound a bit grander than it really is. Most garden sheds don't let the rain in or have a perspex picture window that turns them into a sauna in hot weather.'

Trooping the Colour was a regular posting for some years. It was always rather a mystery why I was asked to do it. The BBC had tried all manner of commentators – some of them retired army officers – but none passed muster with GOC London District and his high command. So, I suspect in a fit of pique, the BBC dispatched me to have dinner with him at his grand official residence in Chelsea. If the army thought the others were substandard, try this one for size. Someone with no experience of the army and its labyrinthine ways who was also rumoured to be a bit of a lefty, certainly so far as the BBC Outside Broadcast department was concerned. That was, of course, a rather meaningless phrase given that Oswald Mosley would have been branded a bit of a lefty in the eyes of some members of the department's staff.

The evening went really rather well after a bit of a shaky start.

GOC: 'Any family connections with the army?'

Robson: 'My dad was in the Scots Guards.'

GOC: 'Would I have known him?'

Robson: 'Best he made was sergeant in North Africa before the war, but he was broken to the ranks twice for insubordination.'

GOC: 'Another scotch?'

The army's main complaint about the BBC coverage of what

they prefer to call the Queen's Birthday Parade was that we put too much emphasis on the ceremonial skills of the soldiers taking part and not enough on the real soldiering they were trained to do. I told them that if they gave me access to the real soldiers who'd be taking part in the parade, I was sure I could find good stories to point up the fact that they spent most of their time in Northern Ireland, the Balkans or the Gulf rather than in the relative safety of Horse Guards Parade.

A young captain from one of the Guards regiments sitting next to me was summarily attached to the production team and told to sort it. During dinner he leaned closer to explain that he'd promised his girlfriend he'd take her to New York the following morning. If I'd cover for him for a couple of days, he'd do the business the minute he got back. I realized this was a chap I could work with, and he was as good as his word.

Trooping the Colour is a bit of a mongrel in comparison with most great state events. (Although I was careful not to make the point as the port was passed round that evening in Chelsea.) Its origins lie in two very ancient ceremonies. On the eve of battle the Colour, the standard of the regiment, would be trooped through the ranks so that it could be more easily recognized by the men as their rallying point. And in the eighteenth century it was the custom for the guards and sentries of the royal palaces and other important buildings in the capital to be mounted on the parade ground at Horse Guards. The two were combined as a celebration of the monarch's official birthday in 1748, and became an annual event abandoned only during the two World Wars and a national rail strike in 1955.

The sovereign only regularly took the salute in person from the reign of Edward VII, and it wasn't until 1914 that the parade was beefed up on the orders of George V to make it a grander display for the increasing number of spectators. That was the first time the King rode at the head of his guards down the Mall to Buckingham Palace behind the massed bands, although I've heard commentators describing that scene and explaining with assured certainty the many centuries of ceremonial tradition it represents.

We get a rehearsal for Trooping the week before, and that's often as much fun as the event itself. It is the Garrison Sergeant Major's morning. He's the Warrant Officer in charge of ceremonial in the capital, and a particularly fine example of the breed was GSM WO1 Alan G. 'Perry' Mason MVO MBE, Coldstream Guards. A giant of a man, he would stand ramrod straight, a brooding presence by the arch of Horse Guards. If he spotted a mistake, which he always did, there would be a bellowed command and then a terrible silence as he marched out onto the square to within an inch of the young officer who'd got it wrong.

'Permission to interrupt, Sah. You're a bleedin' disgrace, Sah.'

At that moment every man present knew he'd spend most of the next week on the parade ground at Chelsea Barracks until they all got it right.

It used to be said of Perry Mason that an order he shouted on Horse Guards could be heard in Trafalgar Square. The year a particularly unpopular Director of Music of one of the Household Cavalry regiments fell off his horse at the rehearsal, I'm sure there would have been people coming to attention in Hampstead. When Perry Mason retired, I heard he went to run a corner newsagents in Eastbourne. Heaven help anyone who didn't come in to collect their ordered copy of the *Daily Telegraph* or whose shoes weren't polished to reflect the sky when they asked for a quarter of boiled sweets.

The Birthday Parade is much tougher for the director than for the commentator. This is a broadcast where he would throw away the camera script at his peril. Dozens of commands, hundreds of individual pieces of parade ground drill, all to be captured in close up on camera in a whirling, complex choreography of ritualized warfare and a glittering spectacle of scarlet and gold. For the commentator, the main pitfalls are to do with phraseology. Volcanic are the retired army officers who hear a pitiful commentator mix up the Field Officer in Brigade Waiting with the Major of the Parade. Incandescent are the Lieutenant-Colonels consigned to old folks' homes in Worthing who suspect that you've called it The Escort TO the Colour before the Colour has actually been put in its charge. It should, of course, have been The Escort FOR the Colour.

I once received a letter in spidery hand from a retired officer suggesting that a spell in the Tower would be altogether too good for me because I'd omitted to mention, as the Colour was lowered in salute as it passed the Queen, that the proper term for the movement was The Flourish. On the off-chance that his medication kicked in sufficiently to overcome the apoplexy and he's lived to read this book, yes, I do know that when the Colour is raised again the proper term is The Recover.

After the first of my broadcasts, the GOC and his staff invited themselves to Television Centre and suggested we should have a debriefing. This was a nervous moment for the commentator, more frightening than the live transmission itself. What had I got wrong? The BBC sent me an off-air tape before the meeting so I could review my mistakes and fall on my sword. When it came to it, I hadn't made many. The army had one or two minor quibbles – the King's Troop Royal Horse Artillery rank rather than trot, I seem to remember was one of them – but overall I got a rather better rating that year than the Secretary of State for Defence, who at the time was mucking about with ancient regiments again. I kept the job. In fact, when I suggested that next year I'd like to make the commentary more user-friendly to the 99.8 per cent of our audience who weren't retired army officers, the assembled army command agreed wholeheartedly.

'What we've been saying all along. We're all in the public relations business these days, y'know.'

For some years I kept up an uneasy truce with the army, renegotiated each year over lunch at Simpson's in the Strand when I'd entertain the officer in charge of the parade. I'd ask him about his career and his family, and whether or not he was nervous about having just one chance to get it right when the Queen was sitting there mentally making a note to check if there was a vacancy on the border between Afghanistan and Pakistan for somebody of his grade. He would ask me about the tricky moments in the ceremonial, because of course I'd done the event more often than he had. Occasionally, we'd negotiate some minor change in the proceedings to suit the television coverage which, if it worked, became tradition. Whether or not these things were ever run past Her Majesty, I never discovered.

I was always pleasantly surprised by the Lieutenant-Colonels who tucked into the roast beef at Simpsons. Their bosses in the high command were often supercilious and generally, if silently, disapproving of this northern oik who'd been foisted on them. But the serving officers whose turn had come to take charge of the parade were a different breed. They stood not a bit on ceremony (off the parade ground at any rate), and always seemed to have a well tuned and frequently wicked sense of humour. They were the new army and most didn't relish the fact that the Birthday Parade would probably be a watershed in their career, marking the end of operational soldiery and the start of the short walk from Horse Guards Parade to a desk in the Ministry of Defence building in

Whitehall. That was the only road to promotion. For myself, I didn't want promotion. I was entirely happy to keep on turning out each June to wish the Queen a happy official birthday.

Having got the job of commentating on Trooping the Colour because of luck and a fit of BBC pique, some years later I lost it for very similar reasons. This time the bad luck was that the Birthday Parade clashed with a particularly important recording of *Gardeners' Question Time*. I had to choose. GQT was fifty-two programmes a year and Trooping the Colour only one, so the freelance choice was relatively easy. I told the Outside Broadcast department that, regrettably, Her Majesty would have to manage without me that year. But turning down the chance to do a major royal event being the broadcasting equivalent of high treason, the BBC had another fit of pique and I wasn't asked back.

Always having a tendency to look on the bright side, at the time I consoled myself with the thought that at least I wouldn't have to work with the double-barrelled pompous ass who'd recently taken over as head of department. But the truth is I still miss the buzz of those long hours of dangerously live broadcasting, sitting in a cramped, overheated shed with the same ancient lip ribbon microphone once used by the likes of Richard Dimbleby and John Snagge, and painting a word picture of some of the most glorious interludes of British life. When, occasionally, I watch programmes such as the Birthday Parade or Remembrance Sunday, all these years later I still can't help noticing the mistakes, but not having been consigned to an old folks' home in Worthing quite yet, I never send nasty letters complaining about them.

CHAPTER TWENTY-ONE
BITING THE HAND THAT FEEDS

I've had two serious problems writing this book. You may think there are more, but I'm owning up to two. The first is that I'm terrible with dates, as you've probably noticed in the general lack of them. Having said that, I managed rather better than the ageing rock star who, when invited to write his autobiography, had to put an advertisement in the *NME* asking anyone who knew where he was or what he was doing between 1968 and 1972 to get in touch with him. The second problem is that I've hardly ever bothered to keep examples of the programmes I've made with which one day to bore the grandchildren. So such stories as have crept into the book crawled unassisted from under the cobwebbed eaves of memory.

But, as I was stirring up the dust, I came across all manner of bits and pieces. The half bus tickets, cuttings and notes on the back of cigarette packets that, for some reason, have been dropped into the memory bin during the past thirty-odd years. Random images. People I interviewed decades ago staring back at me from the party that's in full swing in the personal film library. Eric Burdon of the Animals chatting to Dr Beeching, who's saying that, yes, he has one regret about the railways he closed down in the 1960s and 1970s – that he didn't shut down the bloody lot. And Eric saying what a pleasant change it had been to be interviewed by someone who knew sod all about his music. In another corner, the Dalai Lama is in animated conversation with the one-time Glasgow gangster Jimmy Boyle. Over here the mountaineer Doug Scott compares notes about spiritual revelations with Iris Murdoch, and Sarah Miles swaps stories with Bill Clinton. Prince Charles is getting some tips for Camilla from Brigitte Bardot; Nelson Mandela is learning the complexities of the offside trap from Franz Beckenbauer. Barbara Cartland has just arrived with Michael Foot, and Charlton Heston is comparing the finer points of pump action shotguns with Melvyn Bragg. And then they all look up and raise a glass to toast Robson's luck.

Because, above all, I have been lucky. Any aspiring nineteen year old from Newcastleton who tried to do the same thing today would probably end up on a media studies course at some university like Sunderland or Accrington. (If there isn't a University of Accrington, you can bet your life there will be soon.) He would be like any one of the hundreds of students who write to me every year asking for a break in broadcasting. And in all honesty I would have to tell him what I tell them, that for all the explosion of channels and jolly new media, paid jobs in radio and television are still as hard to find as hens' teeth. Unpaid jobs are easier. There are any number of companies which will happily let students work for nothing or, at best, wages that make the dole look generous, so long as they also pay all their own expenses and don't expect any chance of a permanent job. Of course, it's not exploitation because they call it work experience. The upshot of all this is that broadcasting has much in common with prostitution. The professional bit of the industry is diminished because there are altogether too many enthusiastic amateurs.

The people who really should be on media studies courses are the broadcasters. Proper media studies courses should address the problems that are steadily eroding the quality and credibility of a medium that has such potential to be a standard bearer for, and a valued part of, a more thoughtful society.

Fat chance. The regulator, Ofcom, cravenly gives in to the bosses of ITV, and allows them to enhance their profits by slashing their commitment to regional broadcasting and public service. We'll have to wait and see what the BBC's new governing trust will do, but if it's running true to form it will continue to advance the march of political correctness while at the same time plunging still further into the lowest common denominator ratings war with commercial television. The owners and managers of the television networks may claim that we have the best broadcasting in the world, but I'm afraid these days that's not saying much.

But before this becomes the longest application for a P45 in history, I'm not saying there was once a halcyon golden age or that what we past-our-sell-by-dates tend to think of as the good old days of broadcasting were necessarily better. We often made bad programmes then, too – worthy, boring, uninspired. But at least we made fewer of them (if I'm allowed to wear that as a badge of honour) because there was less broadcasting about. It was a diversion rather than an obsession.

The other great advantage we had in that vague 'then' was that programme making was driven by ideas, not fashion, and certainly not to a formula laid down by that creature of the broadcasting swamp, the head of ratings, whose only values are how many, how big and how long can we get away with it. What keeps the head of ratings in a job is a vague notion of viewer choice. Five terrestrial channels obviously not being anywhere near enough, we've been treated to hundreds of extra satellite channels to make up for their deficiencies. And what does all that 'choice' amount to when we strip away the flim-flam? A bit of specialist sport, a revolving door system of movie repeats, and dozens of channels of low-grade rubbish that are hard to tell apart. Which is no choice at all.

Yes, there's Discovery and National Geographic and the History Channel and Al Jazeera and Sky News, but the vast majority of the stuff on offer is cheap junk. Channels that try to sell us Ratneresque jewellery and exercise bikes. Channels specializing in social inadequates shouting at each other and, when the show's going really well, hitting each other. Freakshow channels that leave no deformity or obesity unturned. Many of my broadcasting colleagues – mainly the ones who produce 'product' for the septic tank channels – will be flicking through the dictionary of broadcasting to the 'elitism' word. They'll be muttering that I'm trying to turn the clock back to an imagined Shangri-la of Reithian paternalism when the broadcasters knew best and provided programmes that were uplifting, educational and good for people.

Two points. One. What's wrong with that if the alternative is the corrosive mix of flatulent drivel that fills 90 per cent of the airwaves today? And, two, how can a chap who makes programmes with a talking dog possibly be accused of elitism?

Hobby horse returned to stable, dog to kennel, let's get back to business. What I hope this canter through three decades of programme making has scotched is any idea that broadcasting is glamorous – all students on media studies courses take note. It's certainly varied, often challenging, but glamorous it ain't. Continuing the aforementioned comparison with prostitution, filming (which you'd imagine to be the glamorous bit of the job) is in reality 95 per cent hanging about on street corners and 5 per cent frantic activity. Many weeks I spend more time on the M6 than I do in the garden, usually moving so slowly that I'd have time to weed the central reservation. Then there's the time we spend in hotels. Look out for my next book – *The Bad Hotel Guide* – soon to be published in fourteen volumes.

There was a time when I quite looked forward to jumping on a plane to jet off to some film trip or other in Spain or America or the Far East. But the realization soon dawned that I was camping out among the plastic delights of airport terminals and sitting with my knees under my chin in steerage for rather longer than I was spending on location. If I'd ever been an inside broadcaster, I might have qualified for business class, but as a cannon fodder freelance I was just lucky not to be sent as air freight.

Maybe it's natural that the only flights you ever remember are the ones that took you closest to your maker, but in the past thirty years broadcasting assignments have had me on speaking terms with him on more occasions than I care to recall. A flight out of Budapest on a brush-painted plane, pride of the Hungarian state airlines fleet, was vibrating so much on take-off that the rivets started to fall out of the ceiling lining. There was an attempt in a rather posher British Airways jet to land in a crosswind at Gibraltar. We'd got low enough to be able to read the brand labels on the washing strung out beside the runway when the captain aborted the attempt, the plane sat on its tail, and by prayer power alone got back to 8,000 feet.

'Most dreadfully sorry about that,' says the Douglas Fairbanks soundalike captain, 'every warning light in the cockpit was going off – windshear, the lot.'

Oh, that's all right then.

If my fear of flying is boring you, feel free to skip the next paragraph, but I've got to tell you about the flight back from the Isle of Man to Blackpool Airport in a small plane which, the moment it was airborne, became a shuttlecock in a hailstorm. The captain on this occasion was blunter in his analysis. 'We really shouldn't be up here,' says he. And there was nothing in that remark with which I could disagree. The flight normally takes about half an hour, but the tailwinds were so strong that day that we made it in about seventeen minutes. I'm sure we were somewhere over Leeds by the time the pilot managed to haul its nose into the wind for landing. We'd been recording *Gardeners' Question Time* that trip, and to this day I still have the imprint of Pippa Greenwood's fingernails in the back of my hand. As we stumbled, shaking and gibbering, into what passes for a passenger terminal at Blackpool, we became aware of the stares of the couple of hundred people who were about to board a jolly holiday flight to Tenerife or some such. Having seen the state we were in, I suspect several of them decided to holiday at home that year.

But enough of this digressive pterygophobia. Assuming nobody from BBC, ITV or Ofcom has read this book, there's still work to do. I've got a fairly average week coming up – Monday with a dog on a string to the Scottish Borders, Tuesday and Wednesday *Gardeners' Question Time* in Merseyside and Shropshire (should be able to finish the central reservation weeding south of Preston), and on Thursday start a new film about the Howgill Fells. On Friday I'm supposed to be seeing a very keen researcher who wants to pick my brains about a new BBC 1 series on the subject of mountains. She was supposed to come and see me last Friday as well, but she got lost somewhere near Ambleside. Which probably doesn't bode well for the venture. On Saturday I am inaugurating a new long-distance walk because they couldn't get anybody famous to do it, and later giving a talk at the Borders Book Festival about the history of the England–Scotland border (and offending any Ruritanian Scottish Nationalists who happen to cross my path). Then on Sunday a day at home writing a treatment for a great new series I've come up with to celebrate my sixtieth birthday – *Round Britain on a Bus Pass*. Nobody's bought it yet, but they will, they will.

OK, catalepsy, do your worst.

INDEX